Presented To: DB

Dimas Daniel Benitez-Lopez Garcia

Date:

October 29, 2008

From: Yaya

Little Boys Bible Storybook

for

Mothers and Sons

Text copyright © 1999 by Carolyn Larsen
Illustrations copyright © 1999 by Caron Turk

New Kids Media™ is published by Baker Publishing Group,
Grand Rapids, Michigan
www.bakerbooks.com

Tenth printing, September 2005

Printed in the United States of America

ISBN 0-8010-4433-2

Little Boys Bible Storybook

for

Mothers  Sons

Carolyn Larsen

Illustrated by Caron Turk

Published in
association with

Little Boys Bible Storybook Contents

Dear Moms,

I had two daughters before my son was born. I remember people saying, "Boys are so different from girls, you'll see!" I didn't believe them because one of my daughters was an absolute daredevil and I didn't see how a boy could be any more energetic than she was. However, they were right. It's hard to explain how—but boys are definitely different to raise than girls are. That's why Caron Turk and I have tried to make this book a little more active, maybe a little more "rough-and-tumble" than the *Little Girls Bible Storybook*.

We hope the stories and illustrations in this book provide a chance for you and your son to see into the hearts of some well-loved Bible characters. Of course, we don't really know what those people actually felt or how they approached some of the situations they were in, but by thinking about what they may have felt, we can understand some of the lessons they learned from their experiences. We hope this book helps your son realize that these were real people with problems, joys, successes and failures—people like us!

Caron has created a spunky little boy angel who is hiding in every illustration. Often, his buddy, a little daredevil lizard is with him. You and your son will have fun looking for the two of them.

My hope is that this book will bring familiar Bible stories to life for you and your son, and that the questions and thoughts in the *Becoming a Man of God* section will be good conversation starters for the two of you. I'm sure your son will love hearing about your childhood memories and experiences.

God bless you and your son as you read *The Little Boys Bible Storybook for Mothers and Sons*.

Carolyn Larsen

That's What Little Boys are Made Of

A big, goofy-looking brown bear scooped honey into his mouth as fast as he could shovel it. When the earth under his feet began to shake the bear dove behind a rock, peeking out at the swirling dust. The bear didn't know it, but God himself was moving the dirt! He was shaping it into his last and best creation—Adam, the very first man.

Adam stretched his arms and wiggled his fingers—
everything worked! He jumped up and raced through the
garden, checking out everything God had made for him.
He skipped stones across a lake. He climbed a tree and
hung upside down. What fun Adam had!

But, just a little while later Adam slumped on the
ground pulling blades of grass and tossing them into a
stream. "What's the matter, son?" God asked.

"I don't know. I guess I'm bored," Adam sighed.

"Hmmm, well, would you like to name the animals?" God asked, trying to think of something fun. "They all need names and you can decide what to call each one. Maybe you'll find one to be your buddy." So God marched the animals by and Adam made up names for each one. But when he finished, he plopped down on the ground again.

"I know what the problem is," God whispered. "You're lonely!"

"I'm what?"

"Lonely. You need someone to talk with and do things with. Someone who is more like you than the animals are." God made Adam fall asleep and he took one of Adam's ribs and used it to make Eve, the first woman.

You will be best friends..... ♥

"Wake up now, my son," God whispered. Adam opened his eyes and saw a brand new, beautiful creature. "This is Eve," God said. "I made her to be your friend and your wife. You both are a lot like me—you can think, and talk, make decisions, and work together. I know you'll be very happy!"

Based on Genesis 1—2

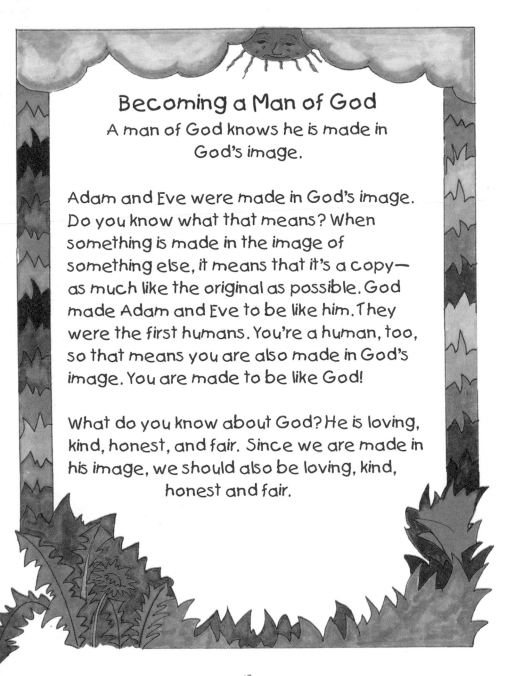

Becoming a Man of God

A man of God knows he is made in God's image.

Adam and Eve were made in God's image. Do you know what that means? When something is made in the image of something else, it means that it's a copy—as much like the original as possible. God made Adam and Eve to be like him. They were the first humans. You're a human, too, so that means you are also made in God's image. You are made to be like God!

What do you know about God? He is loving, kind, honest, and fair. Since we are made in his image, we should also be loving, kind, honest and fair.

Mom's Touch

Share with your son what are your favorite things to do. Crafts? Sports? Reading? Then talk about someone who has different interests or is really good at other kinds of things. Talk about how every person is different because we are all made in God's image—just the way he wants us to be!

      Encourage your son by telling him of a time you noticed him acting in a way that was loving, kind, honest, or fair. Pray with him that you will both be good images of God to those around you.

A Verse to Remember

As the Spirit of the Lord works within us, we become more and more like him and reflect his glory even more.

2 Corinthians 3:18

At First Bite

"Adam! Adam!" Eve's excited voice blasted through the quiet garden. Adam could hear her running, pushing aside branches, and stumbling over bushes.

"Over here, Eve," he called. He stepped out from behind a bush just in time for Eve to crash into him. "Ugh! What's wrong?" he moaned as he picked himself up from the ground.

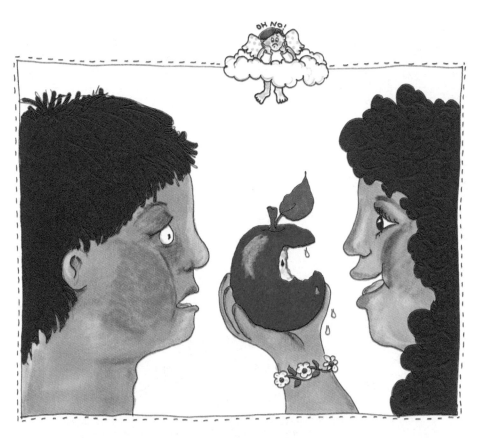

"Taste this—it's great!" Eve cried, shoving a half-eaten piece of fruit in his face. Thick, golden juice ran down her arm, dripping into a little puddle on the ground.

Adam's breath caught in his throat. His stomach twisted into a ball of fear. "T-t-t-that's from the tree God said not to touch, Eve. He said if we even so much as touch it we'll die."

Adam recognized the fruit because he had spent lots of time walking around that tree, looking at it, wondering if it was juicy, wondering why God didn't want him to touch it. Drops of sweat popped out on his forehead because Eve had broken the only rule God gave them.

"Oh phooey, we won't die. That snake over there said that this fruit would make us more like God," Eve whined. "Come on, taste it. I promise you'll thank me."

Adam knew he should just walk away, and that's what he wanted to do. But, Eve held the fruit right under his nose and it smelled so sweet and the juice ran down her arm ... suddenly he grabbed it and stuffed it in his mouth. "M-m-m-m, good," he mumbled. Then a pain shot through his heart as Adam realized he had also broken God's rule.

When God came to the garden later, Adam hid from him. Right away God knew something was wrong, "Oh, Adam, what have you done?"

"Well...I...the snake ..." Adam tried to pass the blame. Finally he blurted out, "It's Eve's fault!"

"Yeah, but ..." Eve started to argue, but when Adam touched her arm she stopped. There was no way out of this. They had disobeyed and that was that.

"I have to punish you," God said sadly, "but remember that I still love you. I will always love you."

Based on Genesis 3

Becoming a Man of God

A man of God takes responsibility for his sin.

Adam and Eve were made in God's image. But they didn't have to always do what he wanted them to do. They could choose to obey or not to obey. In this story, they made a bad choice—they sinned—and God punished them. Sometimes the only way we learn lessons is through punishment. That's not much fun, is it? But we remember the lessons we learn when we've been punished.

Everybody sins—even if we try hard not to we do. When was a time that you did something wrong? Were you punished? How?

Mom's Touch

OK, Mom, it's important for your son to know that you sometimes sin. Tell him about a time when you did something wrong. Were you punished? How did you handle that punishment?

Reinforce to your son that everybody makes mistakes and bad choices. When we do, we should admit it and accept the punishment that is given. We can learn from our mistakes and hopefully not make the same mistake over and over. Remind your son that God loves him no matter what—and so do you!

A Verse to Remember

No matter how deep the stain of your sins, I can remove it. I can make you as clean as freshly fallen snow.

Isaiah 1:18

TATTLETALE

"Why don't you get a real job? How hard can it be to follow a bunch of sissy sheep around?" Cain sneered. Abel just shook his head and went back to watching his sheep.

It seemed to Eve that her boys fought about everything. Actually Cain fought about everything—for some deep-inside-his-heart reason he always tried to prove he was better, stronger, or smarter than his younger brother. She hoped he would outgrow it, but as he got older Cain's jealousy got worse.

One afternoon Cain was working in his fields when he noticed his brother building an altar. "Oh great, that goody-two-shoes is giving an offering to God. Guess that means I have to give one, too. Well, I'm not about to burn up my best grain. I'll just use this scraggly stuff. No one will know anyway."

Cain and Abel each gave their offering to God. But to Cain's surprise God accepted Abel's offering, but rejected his. "WHAT? NO FAIR! NO FAIR!!" Cain shouted. He stomped across the field, kicking down his best grain and mashing it flat.

"Cain, what are you so upset about?" God asked. "Give your offering in the right way and I will accept it, too. Watch it, you're letting sin into your heart!"

The next day Cain was still boiling mad! He came up with a dirty plan. "Hey, bro, I'm sorry I got so mad yesterday," he said sweetly. " Look, I need some help in my field, will you give me a hand?"

"Sure, glad to help," Abel said, with a brotherly slap on Cain's back. But when they got to the field, Cain grabbed a stick and whopped Abel on the head. "Take that you lousy do-gooder!" Abel fell down—dead.

No one saw Cain kill Abel so he jogged home, thinking he had gotten away with murder. Then God asked him, "Cain, where is your brother, Abel?"

"How should I know? It's not my job to know where he is every minute," Cain snapped.

"Abel's blood cries out to me from the ground," God said quietly. "You're guilty of murder. Your punishment is that you must leave your home and wander the earth for the rest of your life!"

Based on Genesis 4:1-12

Becoming a Man of God
A man of God gives God his best!

Does this story sound like God was playing favorites by choosing Abel over Cain? It can sound that way until you look a little deeper. Cain didn't give God the best of his grain. Even worse than that—he didn't give God the best of his heart. He gave an offering only because he saw Abel giving one—not because he was thankful to God or wanted to worship him. Then, he gave God leftovers, not the best of what he had. God wants the best of our love, worship, service, and gifts.

In what ways do you worship God? How can you give him the best of what you have?

Mom's Touch

Your children will learn how important proper worship is by watching how you worship. Talk with your son about what it means to give God your best. Talk about ways to give him the best of your money, time, worship, and praise. Explain to your son how you do this.

Pray with your son that you both can have the right attitudes about worshiping God and giving him your best, not just time and money that is left over from your life.

A Verse to Remember

Great is the LORD! He is most worthy of praise! He is to be revered above all the gods.

Psalm 96:4

Dad's Little Helpers

"Boys, get up! Dad needs your help." Shem, Ham and Japheth slowly sat up and rubbed the sleep from their eyes.

"Why does he need our help so early?" Shem muttered.

"Shh. Don't start the day by complaining," said his mother. "Your breakfast is already on the table."

The boys sat down to eat, not very happy to be awake. Their mother smiled and gently reminded them, "Remember, we're all helping your father build the ark because God told him to build it. We're obeying God."

Just then Noah came in. "That's right, boys. God is tired of the way people are behaving. Everyone is selfish and mean. No one pays any attention to God anymore."

"Yeah, so God is going to wipe out the whole world with a big flood," Ham shouted. He stood on his chair and jumped off, pretending to be drowning.

"This is not a joke, Ham," his mother said sternly. "Everyone is going to die ... except us. That's because your father has led our family to honor and obey God. We have a lot of work to do. Finish your breakfasts."

Soon the whole family was out in the yard. Each boy had a job to do. Shem brought the wood, Ham carried buckets of tar and little Japheth smeared the tar on the boards.

Day after day, week after week, year after year the little family worked. By the time the ark was finished, the boys were grown up and married. Their whole lives they had worked on the ark with their father.

One day after the ark was finished, Japheth came running into the house, "Father, there's hundreds of animals headed this way—hundreds! What do we do?"

"Open the ark. Let them in," Noah answered.

"Grab that food, boys," Mrs. Noah called, "and get your wives. We're going for a boat ride!" The Noah family followed the animals into the ark and God himself closed the big door. Just then rain began to fall.

Based on Genesis 6:1–7:9

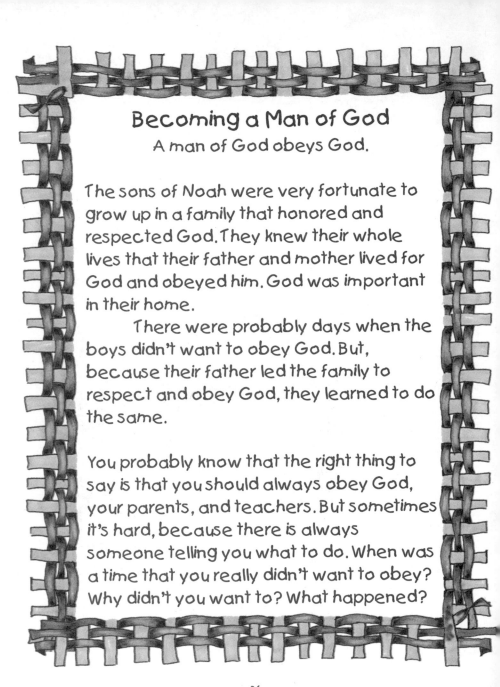

Becoming a Man of God
A man of God obeys God.

The sons of Noah were very fortunate to grow up in a family that honored and respected God. They knew their whole lives that their father and mother lived for God and obeyed him. God was important in their home.

There were probably days when the boys didn't want to obey God. But, because their father led the family to respect and obey God, they learned to do the same.

You probably know that the right thing to say is that you should always obey God, your parents, and teachers. But sometimes it's hard, because there is always someone telling you what to do. When was a time that you really didn't want to obey? Why didn't you want to? What happened?

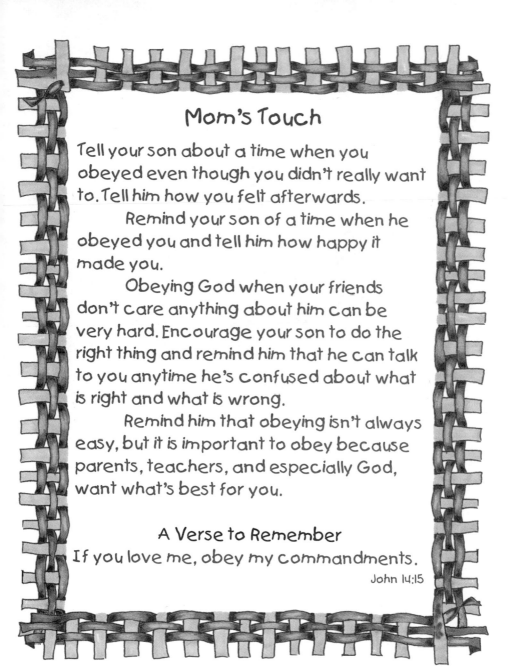

Mom's Touch

Tell your son about a time when you obeyed even though you didn't really want to. Tell him how you felt afterwards.

Remind your son of a time when he obeyed you and tell him how happy it made you.

Obeying God when your friends don't care anything about him can be very hard. Encourage your son to do the right thing and remind him that he can talk to you anytime he's confused about what is right and what is wrong.

Remind him that obeying isn't always easy, but it is important to obey because parents, teachers, and especially God, want what's best for you.

A Verse to Remember
If you love me, obey my commandments.

John 14:15

At first it was a great adventure to be in the big boat. The boys wrestled with the monkeys while their wives played with the bunnies and fed squirrels from their hands. All the while rain pelted the big boat.

One morning Shem smacked Ham on the head and said, "It's your turn to clean the cages!"

"No way, I did it yesterday. It's Japheth's turn!"

"Is not!"

"Is so!"

"Stop fighting!" Mrs. Noah shouted.

"Mom, it's been raining for 30 straight days!" Shem cried. "Look, I made a mark on the wall every morning. THIRTY DAYS! Is it ever going to stop?"

"Every day we wake up to the same old thing—feed the animals, clean the boat, listen to the rain. We're going stir crazy!" Ham added.

"But, remember what's happening outside? Everyone has drowned in the flood—EVERYONE. Stop complaining. Thank God that you're alive," Noah said.

About ten days later Japheth woke everyone up at the end of his night watch, "Hey! Do you hear that?"

His brothers rubbed the sleep from their eyes (much like that long ago day when their mother woke them early to work on the big boat!). "What's the matter with you? I don't hear anything," Shem muttered.

"I know. Isn't it great? The rain stopped. No more pounding on the roof, no more blowing wind. It's quiet!"

"Yippee! Let's get out of this stinky boat!" Ham shouted.

"Slow down, son," Noah laughed. "The water is still pretty deep out there. We'd better wait a while."

When Noah finally said it was safe to leave, the boys whooped and hollered in excitement! "Yippee, yahoo, whooo-eee, hallelu—WHAT'S THAT ???"

All eight people (and a few very smart animals) stopped in their tracks, staring at a beautiful, shimmering arc of bright colors stretched across the sky.

For I will see the rainbow in the cloud and remember my eternal promise to every living being on the earth.

"This rainbow shows my promise to never destroy the world in a big flood again," God explained. "Everytime you see a rainbow, remember how much I love you."

Noah's sons turned around to see their father and mother kneeling in prayer. They dropped to their knees, too, as Noah prayed, "Thank you for saving us God, and thank you for your promise. We will remember your love and we want you to know that we love you, too."

Based on Genesis 7—9

Becoming a Man of God
A man of God remembers to thank God.

When the Noah family first stepped off the big boat, the first thing they did was to thank God. It's so easy to ask God for things: to keep us safe; to make someone well; to help us do something—and it is so important to remember to thank him for answering our prayers.

When you help someone do you like to be thanked? Does it make you want to do even more for them? How do you feel when someone forgets to thank you?

Mom's Touch

Tell your son of a time when you did something for someone and they gave you a big thank you. Then tell him of a time when you weren't thanked. How did you feel each time?

Together make a list of the ways God takes care of you. Thank God for his care. Tell your son of a time when you observed him thanking someone for their help or a gift—without you reminding him to do so. Tell him how proud you are of him when he remembers to do that.

A Verse to Remember

Give thanks to the LORD, for he is good! His faithful love endures forever!

I Chronicles 16:34

The Miracle Baby

"Whew, it's hot today!" Abraham thought, sitting down in the shade of the only tree around. He fanned himself and listened to Sarah working inside their tent. A little heat didn't stop Sarah from making dinner and even stirring up a few treats for the children who were sure to drop by later. Kids loved Abraham and Sarah and since they didn't have any children of their own they had plenty of time to spend with their nieces and nephews.

Abraham looked up at the waves of heat rising from the desert sand. "That can't be someone walking across the desert in this heat. I must be seeing things," Abraham rubbed his eyes and looked again. Soon he could make out three men coming toward him. "Hey," he called. "Come over here in the shade. Sit down and rest for a while!"

"Sarah, bring some water and some food for our guests," Abraham called. As the men ate Sarah's dinner and drank the cool water they talked. "We'll come back at about this time next year," one man said. "By then, Sarah will be the proud mother of a baby boy." This was amazing news since Abraham and Sarah were both very old—too old to have a baby, that's for sure!

Sarah was listening from inside the tent and when she heard what the man said, a quick "harumpff" slipped out before she could slap a hand over her mouth. She looked at her wrinkled hands, fingers bent from arthritis and it suddenly struck her funny to think that her old body could have a baby. She started laughing and didn't stop until tears were spilling down her wrinkled cheeks.

"Why did Sarah laugh?" the stranger asked Abraham. "Does she think this is too hard for God?" Poor old Abraham was in shock himself at the news of becoming a father after all these years. He didn't know what to think. The men left then, but sure enough nearly a year later, Sarah and Abraham were counting the fingers and toes of their newborn son, Isaac.

Based on Genesis 18:1-15; 21:1-7

Becoming a Man of God
A man of God believes God.

Abraham and Sarah tried to always obey God. They trusted him and did whatever he asked them to do, even when what he asked was hard.

They had always wanted a child, but they were both so old now that it seemed impossible. When the man said that Sarah was going to have a baby, Sarah wasn't quite sure at first, but she quickly believed him because when God says he's going to do something, that settles it!

Being able to believe what someone tells you is so important. Has someone ever told you he would do something and then not done it? How did you feel? Did you believe that person the next time he told you he would do something?

Mom's Touch

Share a story about a time when someone disappointed you by not keeping his word. Talk about how hard it was to believe that person the next time.

We can always believe God's promises. How do we know what his promises are? By reading his Word and understanding it.

Help your son understand that sometimes we have to wait a long time for God to do what he says, but that's OK, because we know that if he said he will do something—he will!

A Verse to Remember

Without wavering, let us hold tightly to the hope we say we have, for God can be trusted to keep his promise.

Hebrews 10:23

No More Teasing!

Isaac was Sarah's pride and joy. After all, she had waited a long time for this child. When Isaac was still a little guy his father, Abraham, threw a party for him. Everyone ate and played games. Isaac was the center of attention and enjoying it very much—until his step-brother Ishmael began teasing him—holding a cookie just out of Isaac's reach and whining, "Come on little baby—take it. Why don't you take it, you baby?"

Sarah watched Ishmael's mean game. She heard Isaac's cries, and she got more and more angry. Finally, she threw down the plate she was holding and stomped across the yard to Abraham. "I want that bully out of here. Send Ishmael and Hagar away. That boy will not have any part of your inheritance! It all belongs to Isaac!"

Abraham sadly told Hagar that she and Ishmael had to leave. "No, please don't send us away! I won't tease Isaac anymore. I promise!" Ishmael cried. He didn't want to leave his home and his dad. Abraham didn't want his son to leave, either. But he felt better when God told him not to worry because he would take care of Ishmael and Hagar. God even told him that Ishmael would be the leader of a nation when he grew up.

Abraham gave them water, hugged his son, and sent Hagar and Ishmael away. They wandered around in the wilderness for a long time.

When their food and water were gone Ishmael cried, "I'm thirsty. I want to go home." He got so weak that Hagar was afraid he would die. With tears rolling down her cheeks, she walked away from him and prayed, "God, I can't take it. My son is dying!"

She was crying so hard that she didn't even notice the angel God sent to comfort her. "Hagar," the angel said, "it's OK. God heard Ishmael's cries. He wants you to know that your son will be fine." Hagar opened her eyes and saw a well, filled to the brim with cool, clear water. She got a drink for Ishmael and hugged him tightly. Love spilled from her heart as she thanked God for his care.

Based on Genesis 21:8-21

Becoming a Man of God
A man of God knows God will take
care of him.

Hagar was scared because she thought her
son was going to die. Ishmael's father,
Abraham turned his back on them, so she had
no place left to turn, except to God.
Actually, while Hagar may have felt that she
was at the end of her rope—she was really in
the best possible place. God loves his
children and loves to take care of them. So,
we can talk to him about whatever we need
and he will help us.

What are some ways that God takes care of
you?

Mom's Touch

This is a good opportunity to share some things that concern you. It's healthy for your son to know that adults have worries and concerns, but that you talk to God about them and believe that he will take care of you. Tell him about a specific time when you talked to God about a problem and he took care of you in a special way.

Make a list of the ways God cares for you and your son. Ask your son if there are specific things he would like to talk with God about. Pray together.

A Verse to Remember
You will keep in perfect peace all who trust in you, whose thoughts are fixed on you!

Isaiah 26:3

"Uhh, Dad, We Have a Problem"

"Dad's acting kind of strange today," Isaac thought. Old Abraham was packing a few things for a trip up the mountain, but something wasn't right. Isaac just couldn't put his finger on what it was. "It's not so odd that he wants to make a sacrifice to God. But he doesn't usually ask me to come along. Maybe he just wants me to learn how to do it," Isaac thought.

God will provide, my son

Abraham led a donkey loaded with wood and a pot of fire up the mountain. Isaac ran ahead picking up stones and tossing them as far as he could. Suddenly Isaac knew what was wrong. Usually his dad took a lamb to be the sacrifice. "Father, we forgot ..." before he finished Abraham put a finger to his lips, he knew what Isaac was going to say.

"God will provide, my son," Abraham said quietly.

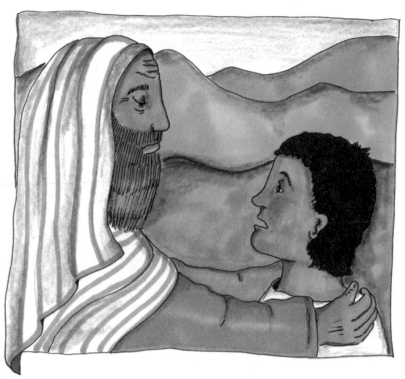

They reached the top of the mountain and Abraham said, "Get some stones, son. We need to build an altar." Father and son worked quietly together. Isaac thought he had never seen his father so tense.

When the altar was built Abraham said, "Come here, son." Isaac's heart filled with fear! His own father tied up his hands and feet and laid him on the altar—HE WAS THE SACRIFICE!

"But Dad ..." Isaac started to cry.

"Shhh. I love you with all my heart Isaac, but I love God more. This is what he told me to do," Abraham was so upset that he could barely get the words out.

He raised his knife to sacrifice his own son when the voice of God's angel stopped him, "Wait. Don't hurt your son. You have shown that you love God more than anything and that is the way it should be."

Isaac didn't even realize he was holding his breath until he heard the angel's voice. Relief spread across his face as his father untied him. They hugged long and hard. Abraham caught a ram that God put in the bushes and together they sacrificed it to God. The sweet prayers of father and son, standing with arms around each other, were filled with praise to the God who would one day sacrifice his only Son.

Based on Genesis 22:1-14

Becoming a Man of God
A man of God loves God most of all!

Isaac learned an important lesson at a young age--don't put anything-ANYTHING-ahead of God. Other things and people may be very important to you, but they should never be more important than God.

Who is important to you? Who do you love a whole bunch? Is that person sometimes more important to you than God?

Mom's Touch

Tell your son how important he is to you and how you thank God every day for him.

Share a time when something seemed more important to you than God—maybe it was a possession or maybe it was a position, such as a job or a part in a play. Maybe it was a person. Talk about how it became more important than God. How did you handle it?

Talk about what is important to your son. Encourage him to share what he really cares about. Talk about ways to keep God in first place.

A Verse to Remember

You are worthy, O Lord our God, to receive glory and honor and power. For you created everything, and it is for your pleasure that they exist and were created.

Revelation 4:11

Boys Will Be Boys

"MOM! Esau hit me!" Jacob screamed. Rebekah came running and found Jacob flat on the ground, Esau holding him down with a foot planted firmly on his chest. She sighed, wondering if her sons would ever outgrow this and be friends. They didn't.

When the boys grew up Jacob was a homebody. He helped Rebekah cook and take care of the house. Esau loved to be out hunting with his father. The brothers were like oil and water—they just didn't mix.

One afternoon Rebekah was cleaning when she heard her husband say, "Esau, I'm old and I'm sick. I know that I won't be around much longer. Since you are my oldest son, I want to give you the family blessing. This honor means you will lead the family after I die. Hunt some wild game, and cook my favorite meal for me. After I eat, I'll give you the blessing."

Rebekah threw down her broom. Years of Esau winning over Jacob and making fun of him welled up in her mother's heart. She knew that she shouldn't favor one son over the other. But she did. She wanted to shout, "Jacob should have that blessing. It's time for him to win!" Instead, she went to Jacob and said, "Your father is ready to give the family blessing to your brother. But, I'm going to get it for you!"

"Oh, right. We're going to make Father think I'm Esau? Did you forget Esau has hairy skin, and mine is smooth?"

"Don't be snippy," Rebekah said tossing goatskins at him. "Put these on your arms so you feel like Esau."

When Jacob went to his father, Isaac was confused, "You sound like Jacob but you feel like Esau."

"I am Esau," Jacob lied. "Give me the blessing."

"May God bless you, may nations serve you, and may you rule over your brothers." It was done. Jacob had stolen Esau's blessing.

As soon as Esau found out what had happened he begged for a blessing, too, "Please Father, you must have a blessing left for me!" But Isaac didn't. Esau angrily threw a chair against a wall. "I'll get even with Jacob!"
Jacob hid behind his mother, scared of Esau's anger. "It's OK, you just have to get away for awhile until he calms down," Rebekah said. Later, she watched as her favorite son left home. He had the blessing, but she wondered, "Will I ever see him again?"

Based on Genesis 27:1–28:6

Becoming a Man of God
A man of God learns from his mistakes.

Whew! This mom and son made a big mistake, didn't they? Deep down inside Jacob and Rebekah knew that it was wrong to steal the family blessing. They made a bad choice—we all do that sometimes. But, if they learned a lesson then it wasn't a wasted experience.

Have you ever been jealous of someone who seems to always have better toys or get better grades or do things that are more fun than anyone else? Have you wanted to get something that you didn't really deserve? Did any of your friends or family get angry with you? What happened?

Mom's Touch

Has your son ever heard you admit that you have made a mistake? Has he heard you apologize to God and to the people who were hurt by your mistake?

Share an experience you had when you made a bad choice or a mistake. What happened? How did you settle the problem?

It's important for your son to realize that everyone makes mistakes so that he isn't too hard on himself when he does. Thank God for his forgiveness and his love.

A Verse to Remember
Though they stumble, they will not fall, for the LORD holds them by the hand.

Psalm 37:24

One Big Happy Family

"Let me outta here! Come on guys, this isn't funny!" Joseph shouted. He tried and tried to climb out of the hole in the ground where his brothers had thrown him.

Noone paid any attention to Joseph's cries. His brothers were fed up with him. He was their dad's favorite son and Jacob didn't try to hide it. He even gave Joseph fancy presents like a rich-looking colorful coat!

Joseph was still screaming and trying to jump out of the hole when some men came by on the way to Egypt. "Hey, we can make some money and get rid of Joseph, too," one brother said. "Let's sell him to those guys to be a slave. We can tell Father that an animal killed him." Before he could say "pyramid" Joseph was in Egypt—the slave of a man named Potiphar.

"Well, this isn't so bad," Joseph thought. He worked hard and was soon put in charge of the whole household. But, one day Mrs. Potiphar got madder than a wet hen because Joseph wouldn't do something she wanted him to do. She told nasty lies about him and poor Joseph ended up in jail!

"Hey, look at Goody-Two-Shoes praying again! Your prayers really work great—look where you are! Ha ha ha!" The other prisoners made fun of Joseph for his faith in God ...until the day two of them had strange dreams. God helped Joseph explain what their dreams meant ...and he was right!

Later God helped Joseph explain Pharaoh's dreams, too. Pharaoh was so happy that he made Joseph second in command over the whole country!

About that time there was a drought in Egypt—no food would grow. But Joseph had planned ahead and saved up food. He sold some to people from other countries.

One day Joseph looked up to see his own brothers waiting to buy food. They didn't recognize Joseph—but he knew them! He could have tried to get even with them, but he didn't. Instead he said, "Hey, it's me, Joseph. I forgive you for trying to hurt me." That's exactly what God wanted him to do!

Based on Genesis 37–45

77

Becoming a Man of God
A man of God forgives.

Joseph's brothers were very mean to him. They didn't care if he had to be a slave for the rest of his life—or even if he died. But when Joseph had the chance to pay them back for the way they had treated him, he didn't. Instead, he was kind and helpful. He forgave them instead of getting even with them.

Has someone ever done something mean to you? What was it? How did you feel? Did you want to get even with them? What happened? How did you feel afterward?

Mom's Touch

Tell your son about a time when someone hurt you. What happened? How did you feel? Did you forgive that person?

Being forgiven is wonderful— and a wonderful thing to do. Remind your son how Jesus forgave the people who crucified him— even while he was hanging on the cross.

Thank God that he is always willing to forgive us for the wrong things we do.

A Verse to Remember

Even if (your brother) wrongs you seven times a day and each time turns again and asks forgiveness, forgive him.

Luke 17:4

One Determined Mama

"I don't care what Pharaoh ordered, no soldiers are taking my baby away!" Jochebed patted Moses' on the back as she paced back and forth across the room. Finally a gentle "b-u-r-r-p" slipped from his lips and he smiled up at her.

"But, Pharaoh ordered that all Hebrew baby boys be killed. How do you expect to save our son?" Moses' father wished he had an answer to his own question.

Maybe he didn't have an answer, but Jochebed did.
"Miriam, hold the baby. I'll be back soon," the determined
mama said. When she came back a while later, her arms
were filled with muddy reeds pulled from the banks of the
Nile River. Miriam quietly watched as her mama's sure
hands wove the reeds together tightly. Soon she had a
little basket—just the right size for the baby to fit inside.
But Miriam didn't understand how a new place to sleep
could help save the baby.

Jochebed hugged baby Moses, humming the little song she always sang as she rocked him to sleep. Then she lay him in the little basket and tucked his favorite toy in beside him.

Jochebed and Miriam carried the sleeping baby to the Nile River and gently set the little basket afloat. "Stay here and watch what happens to him," Jochebed whispered to Miriam. Her heart ached with hope.

The sad mama slowly walked home. Her arms felt so empty with no baby to cuddle and hug.

Meanwhile, Miriam hid behind the reeds on the river bank. Moses' basket floated dangerously close to the place Pharaoh's daughter sometimes came to bathe. Miriam's heart pounded harder and harder—what if she got caught hiding here and what would happen to Moses if Pharaoh's daughter found him? Would he be killed like all the other Hebrew baby boys?

A while later Pharaoh's daughter came to the river. Right away she spotted the floating basket. Miriam could hear her brother crying when the princess opened it.

The princess felt sorry for the baby and wanted to keep him, so Miriam ran to her with an idea. Minutes later, Miriam burst into the house calling, "Momma, the princess found Moses. She's going to raise him as her own son and she needs someone to be his nurse. Hurry Momma, you can take care of him!"

Based on Exodus 2:1-10

Becoming A Man of God
A man of God takes action!

Jochebed didn't want her son to die. She felt so strongly about this that she came up with a plan to keep him alive. Jochebed did what she could and God did the rest.

Sometimes when we have to trust God with how a situation works out ... all we can do is wait patiently. But there are also times when God wants us to use the brains he gave us and do what we can. We should ask God for wisdom and help ... and get busy!

Have you ever been part of a plan for something that needed to be done?

A Mom's Touch

Tell your son about a time when you knew that God was leading you to get involved in a project. Perhaps you helped organize a dinner for someone who didn't have enough food to eat; or maybe you volunteered to teach Sunday School. Talk about how you know the difference between the times when God wants you to "wait patiently" and the times you need to take action.

Ask your son if he has ever wanted to take action about something. What was it? Pray together for the courage and wisdom to take action when God wants you to.

A Verse to Remember

Learn to do good. Seek justice. Help the oppressed. Defend the orphan. Fight for the rights of widows.

Isaiah 1:17

Red Sea PANIC

The minute someone saw the Egyptian army chasing after them the people were in Moses' face and his sister and wife, Miriam and Zipporah watched it all.

"What's going to happen to us? Did you bring us out here to die? We should have stayed in Egypt!" Everywhere Moses looked he saw panicked eyes wide with fear.

Moses understood that the people were confused. God
did ten awesome miracles to get them out of Egypt.
"I know what happened," Moses thought. "Pharaoh must
have realized that without us there was no one to make
bricks and do the other slave work. So, Pharaoh and his
whole army have come to bring us back. What a mess, the
army is coming at us and we're trapped with our backs
against the Red Sea!"

Moses pushed through the crowd of shouting people and climbed onto a big rock where he could be alone. He knelt down and poured out his heart to God. "Are my people going to die here? Are we going to be dragged back to slavery? Dear, God, what is going on?"

Of course, God had a plan. He didn't bring his people to the desert just to leave them alone and let bad things happen. God told Moses exactly what to do.

"Be quiet!" Moses called to the frightened Hebrews. "Watch what God will do to save you!" He lifted his hand over the sea. Immediately the wind began to blow— harder and harder it blew. Mommas held on to babies and daddies held on to mommas. The wind blew so hard that the waters blew apart—two big walls of water stood high. It kept blowing until the ground between the walls was completely dry. "Go on through!" Moses cried. The scared people held back, until one man bravely stepped out, then all the people followed.

It took a long time for all the people to cross, even though they hurried as fast as they could—parents carrying children and young people helping old people.

The Egyptian army raced into the sea, sure that they could catch the Hebrews. But when Moses raised his hand over the sea again, the walls of water crashed down, flooding over the soldiers and chariots. Every Egyptian soldier died in the Red Sea that day, but God kept every Hebrew safe!

Based on Exodus 14

Becoming a Man of God
A man of God works for God.

Way back at the burning bush when God first asked Moses to lead his people to freedom, Moses was scared. He didn't think he could do it. But now, God told him to raise his hand over the sea and Moses did it! He was willing to do whatever God told him to do.

Someday God may ask you to do something that you think is too hard. Remember that he won't ask you to do a job without promising to help you do it!

When have you had to do something that was hard or scary? Why was it scary? Were you able to do it?

Mom's Touch

Share a time when you had to do something that was very difficult for you. Why were you afraid? How did you get through it? How did you feel afterward?

Talk about the way that exercising the muscles in your body makes them stronger. It's the same way with our "spiritual muscles." Trusting God to help us do hard things and seeing how he helps makes our faith grow stronger.

A Verse to Remember
I can do everything with the help of Christ who gives me the strength I need.

Philippians 4:13

And the Walls Come A Tumblin' Down

Moses led the Israelites for many years. When he died God chose Joshua as the new leader. Joshua loved God very much and tried to lead the people to trust him, too.

One time Joshua and the Israelites camped near Jericho, a city that was surrounded by big walls with gates they kept locked up tight. God said to Joshua, "I'm giving you the city of Jericho. Go get it, but be sure to do it the way I tell you."

"God said we can capture Jericho," Joshua announced.

"Alright! We'll attack them so hard that they won't know what hit them!" the Israelites cheered.

"No. We're going to do exactly what God says: March around the city once a day for six days—without saying a word!" Joshua was very firm.

"Huh? We'll look like fools," the people muttered.

"God said it, so we're doing it." The people knew better than to argue with Joshua.

"HA! Look at those crazy Israelites!" the men of Jericho laughed. "What do they think they're gonna do ...shake the walls so hard that they fall down?"

Once a day for six days the Israelite army silently marched around the city then went back to their camp. By the sixth day, the men of Jericho were making so much fun of them that some of the Israelites wondered if Joshua really knew what he was doing.

The seventh day people in Jericho woke up to the sounds of the Israelites marching again. "Why don't they go away?" people wondered, before rolling over and going back to sleep. Some people did notice that the Israelites didn't stop after one time around. "Ahh, it's just some new wrinkle in their silly plan," they thought. Six times Joshua led the people around the city. By then crowds of people were on the walls making fun of the army and throwing water at them. But, even with water dripping into his eyes Joshua kept marching.

"Hey you fools, you're gonna wear out your sandals, or make a rut in the ground with all that marching!" People shouted and threw rotten veggies at the Israelites.

As they started the seventh time around Joshua yelled, "Shout, the Lord has given you this city!"

"Yahoo!!" the Israelites whooped and shouted and the priests blared on their horns. The men on the walls jumped back in surprise—some even fell off when the walls began to crumble and fall to the ground. The Israelites raced over them to capture Jericho. God gave them the city—just as he said!

Based on Joshua 6

Becoming a Man of God
A man of God follows instructions.

Joshua was good at following instructions. He believed that God would help them capture Jericho, but only if they did just exactly what he told them to do.

Following instructions is important. For example, if you help your mom make cookies, but you put in more flour and less margarine than the instructions say, the cookies won't taste very good.

How are you at following instructions? Are you careful to do exactly what you are told to do? What are some instructions that are easy for you? What kind are hard?

Mom's Touch

Explain a time when you didn't follow instructions you were given. What happened? Did you get lost? Lose a game? Get a bad grade in school? Did you learn a lesson from this experience?

Remind your son of a time when he obeyed and followed the instructions you gave him. Tell him how proud you were of him and how happy that made you. Talk with your son about how we know what God's instructions for us are. We can read the Bible and find lots of guidelines for how to live. You can start with the Ten Commandments in Exodus 20.

A Verse to Remember

Love the LORD your God, walk in all his ways, obey his commands, be faithful to him, and serve him with all your heart and all your soul.

Joshua 22:5

Thank God for Second Chances!

"EEEEIIII YOOOOO!" Samson jerked the angry, roaring lion high up in the air and tossed it out of his way. Then he flipped his long black hair over his shoulder and went on his way. NO ONE ... not even a full-grown madder-than-anything lion messed with Samson. He was the strongest man in the world! No one could match his strength ... but he did have one weakness. Samson loved pretty girls. He liked to tease them and he liked it when they teased back. This weakness was going to get him in big trouble!

Samson fell head-over-heels for a pretty Philistine girl named Delilah. The problem was that the Philistines hated Samson. (Once he had killed a bunch of Philistines, just using a donkey's jawbone and the rest of them wanted to get even!). The sneaky Philistines came up with a plan, "Find out where Samson's strength comes from and we'll pay you big money!" they told Delilah. Right away money-hungry Delilah started whining and nagging Samson to tell her the secret of his strength.

Samson teased her, giving goofy answers—"New ropes will hold me" or "Tie me up with seven bowstrings and I'll be as weak as anyone." Each time Delilah did what he said, and called the Philistines, but each time Samson flexed his muscles and escaped.

"You don't love me," Delilah pouted. "If you did you'd tell me the truth."

Samson couldn't stand to have her mad at him, "My strength comes from my long hair. It's never been cut because I was dedicated to God as a baby. If my hair were cut, my strength would be gone."

Aha! Now Delilah had him! She waited for Samson to fall
asleep, then she called, "Come in my Philistine friends, and
bring your money. Cut his hair off and Samson is yours!"
Strands of long, beautiful hair fell to the floor. Samson
woke up while they were tying his arms and he tried to flex
his muscles ... but nothing happened. Laughing at him, the
Philistines poked his eyes out and dragged him off to
prison. Delilah stretched out on her bed and counted her
money.

A while later the Philistines paraded Samson around at a big party. The people laughed and made fun of him. (No one noticed that his hair had grown back.)

"O God, help me one last time to beat the Philistines," Samson prayed. Then he put each hand on one of the giant pillars that held up the building and pushed with all his might. Almost in slow motion the pillars cracked and broke in half. The building crashed down, killing Samson and all the Philistines—more than he had killed in his whole life.

Based on Judges 16

Becoming a Man of God

A man of God doesn't let anything come
between him and God.

Samson blew it! As a young child he was
dedicated to serve God. He didn't always
behave in a way that showed God was
important to him ... especially in this story. His
weakness for pretty girls came between him
and God and ended up being his downfall.
Thankfully, Samson realized his sin later,
repented and served God once again.

Is there anything or anyone that you really,
really like and that could become more
important to you than God? What is it? How do
you make sure that you keep God in the most
important place in your life?

Mom's Touch

Have you ever struggled with something or someone becoming more important to you than God? Tell your son about it and how it affected your relationship with God. How did you get things back on the right track? Is that thing or person still important to you?

Tell your son that it's OK to care about people or things, but he should never let something become so important that it pulls him away from God.

Pray with your son that you will both be able to keep God in the center of your lives, no matter what.

A Verse to Remember

Do not worship any other gods besides me.

Exodus 20:3

Do You Hear Something?

Late at night Samuel stretched out on his cot and thought about his momma, "I wonder what she did today. I wonder if she misses me." But his thoughts always ended with a prayer, "Dear God, thank you for my mom. I miss her, but I know she loves you and she wants me to know you, too." Then little Samuel rolled over and went to sleep. He knew that tomorrow would be a busy day—they were all busy. Samuel lived in the temple and helped Eli the priest as he to learned how to be a priest himself.

GOD BLESS YOU SAMUEL

"I'm tired, it's been a long day. I didn't know a priest had to
know so much," Samuel thought. "Eli even went to bed
early tonight. I hear him snoring in his room."

Samuel fell asleep right away and was deep into
dreamland when he heard, "Samuel, Samuel!" He dragged
himself awake and stumbled into Eli's room.

"Yes, Eli, what do you need?"

The funny thing was, Eli was asleep and Samuel
woke him. "I didn't call you Samuel, go back to bed," Eli
mumbled.

"I must have been dreaming," Samuel thought, climbing back into bed. He fell asleep quickly, but was jolted awake again when he heard, "Samuel, Samuel!" He tumbled out of bed and ran to Eli's room, stubbing his toe on a chair as he rounded the corner.

"I'm here. What do you need?" he said as he rubbed his throbbing toe.

"Why did you wake me again? I didn't call you. Go back to bed." Eli turned his back and didn't say another word.

Samuel was confused, "Is Eli playing a trick on me, or what?" He tried to fall asleep again but a few minutes later he heard the voice again. "Samuel, Samuel."

"OK, this isn't funny anymore," Samuel thought as he marched into Eli's room.

"Yes, Eli. What do you need?" he asked, maybe a little too loudly.

The old priest sat up. Now he knew what was happening, so he told Samuel what to do.

Samuel, Samuel..."

Samuel went back to bed, but he didn't go to sleep this time. He just lay very still and waited. Before long he heard, "Samuel, Samuel."

"Yes, Lord, I'm listening," he answered, just as Eli had told him to do. "Eli was right! It is God calling me!" Samuel was amazed, "I'm just a kid, why does God want to talk to me?" He listened carefully to everything God said. That night Samuel learned an important lesson about listening when God calls.

Based on 1 Samuel 3

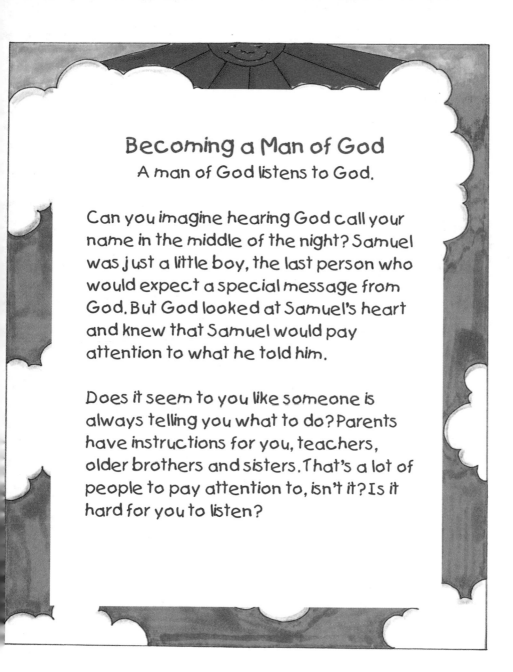

Becoming a Man of God
A man of God listens to God.

Can you imagine hearing God call your name in the middle of the night? Samuel was just a little boy, the last person who would expect a special message from God. But God looked at Samuel's heart and knew that Samuel would pay attention to what he told him.

Does it seem to you like someone is always telling you what to do? Parents have instructions for you, teachers, older brothers and sisters. That's a lot of people to pay attention to, isn't it? Is it hard for you to listen?

Mom's Touch

Each of us has had an experience of listening with all of our attention as well as times when we have only partially paid attention. The partial attention times usually get us in trouble. Tell your son about a time when you learned something important because you listened. Tell him about a time when you didn't listen, and later wished that you had.

Sometimes our world is so noisy that it's hard to hear the important things. Talk about the importance of a quiet time with God. Take time together to read God's Word and talk to him, and also to just be quiet and let his Word sink into your hearts.

A Verse to Remember

Come here and listen to me! I'll pour out the spirit of wisdom upon you and make you wise.

Proverbs 1:23

No Fear!

"I'm not scared!" David said firmly. "I mean it. I'm not scared of that big, ugly giant!" He stood with his feet spread apart and his hands on his hips. "How can all of King Saul's soldiers just let that big creep keep on makin' fun of them ... and of God?"

That's exactly what the soldiers had been doing. Twice a day for forty days Goliath shouted, "Hey you Israelite chickens, send someone out to fight me. Come on. Winner takes all!" No one volunteered.

Everytime David heard Goliath's shouts he got mad. "How can all these big, brave, soldiers be scared of him, when I'm not ...I'm just a kid!"

Suddenly David felt a hand grab his shoulder and squeeze it hard. "What are you doing here, you little show-off?" It was David's older brother and he was MAD! "Just go home, you don't belong here."

"I'll go—but not home!" David answered. He marched into King Saul's tent and announced, "I'll fight the giant!"

King Saul was excited to finally have a volunteer . . . until he looked at the skinny little boy. "What chance would you have against a 9-foot-tall giant?" But, he had to admit that the kid look determined. "Well, OK, but at least wear my armor," he said.

David put it on, but the armor was so heavy that he couldn't take a step or lift his arms. "Get me outta this tin can!" he cried. "I gotta do this my way!"

As David went down the hill, he picked up some rocks, and dropped one into his slingshot.

King Saul's soldiers ran to the top of the hill and watched the brave young man. "He's crazy!" "Nah, he's just stupid!" They didn't know WHAT to think.

When Goliath saw the kid with the slingshot and shepherd's staff, he was M-A-D! He glared at David and flexed his muscles and pounded his spear into the ground. David didn't even flinch!

As he got closer to Goliath, David swung his slingshot around and around over his head. It seemed to hypnotize the giant. Finally, David let go and the rock flew out of the sling and shot through the air. It landed right on Goliath's forehead. THUD! The 9-foot-tall giant looked totally shocked as he fell to the ground.

The Philistine soldiers saw their hero fall and they hightailed it down the hillside. The Israelite soldiers shouted and cheered, "He won! The little guy won!"

Based on 1 Samuel 18

Becoming a Man of God
A man of God trusts God's power.

This scene must have looked pretty funny. All of King Saul's big brave soldiers stood around watching as a young boy went to fight the giant that they were all afraid of. Why were none of them able to fight Goliath? Because they didn't believe they had God's power to help them.

Have you ever had to do something that was really hard? What was it? Why was it scary? Did you ask God to help you? How do you know that he did help?

Mom's Touch

One way that your little guy will learn to trust in God's power is by seeing you trust God in your everyday life. He must learn to not only call on God in a crisis, but to develop an everyday relationship with him.

Share a story with your son about a time when you knew without a doubt that God's power was helping you.

Ask your son what kinds of situations he finds difficult. Talk through what it is that frightens him. Pray together for God's help and for your son to KNOW when God is helping him. Remember to thank God for his help and constant care.

A Verse to Remember
The LORD is good. When trouble comes, he is a strong refuge.

Nahum 1:7

Loyal Buddies

"Jonathan, what have I done wrong? Why does your dad want to kill me?" David was scared. King Saul had chased him around the countryside and even thrown sharp spears at him—and David didn't know what he had done.

"Oh come on, don't you think you're overreacting?" Jonathan asked. He leaned back and heaved a pebble high into the air. A few minutes later it landed with a soft splash in the nearby lake.

"Dad wouldn't hurt you. He's probably just playing around," Jonathan couldn't believe that his dad would really hurt David. "After all, he knows you're my best friend. Besides, Dad tells me everything he's planning to do. He hasn't said anything about being mad at you."

"Exactly, he knows we're good friends. He wouldn't tell you that he wants me dead because that would hurt you. But, I'm telling you that I am just one spear throw away from death!" David pounded his fist on his open palm to show how serious this matter was. "I have a plan," David said, "a way we can find out what he's thinking." David explained his idea to Jonathan.

Be Careful David....

The next day Jonathan sat down to eat a big dinner with his father. Everything was fine for awhile, then King Saul shouted, "Where's David?"

"He went to see his family," Jonathan said softly.

"Go get him so I can kill him," King Saul shouted. He jumped up so fast that his chair flew back against the wall. "As long as he's alive, you'll never be king!"

Jonathan was sad. Now he knew that his father really did want to hurt David.

Jonathan went out to the field where David was hiding and shot three arrows. Then he sent a servant to get the arrows, "That one arrow is still ahead of you," he shouted to the boy. That was the sign that meant King Saul wanted to kill David. When the boy left, David came out and the two friends hugged. Tears rolled down their faces because they knew that David had to leave and they might never see each other again.

Based on I Samuel 20

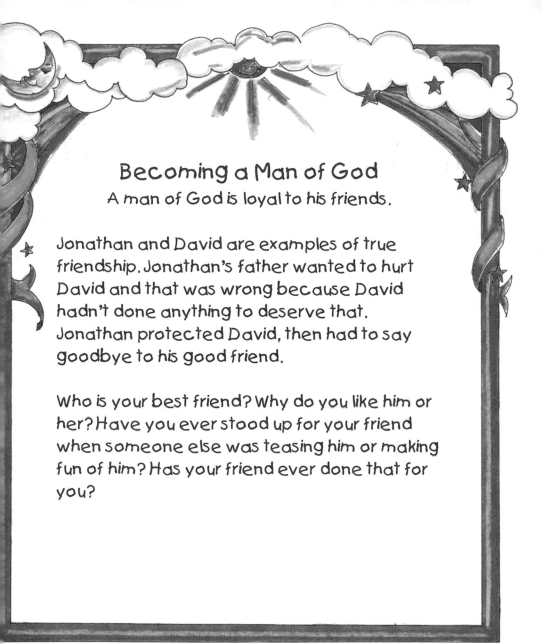

Becoming a Man of God
A man of God is loyal to his friends.

Jonathan and David are examples of true friendship. Jonathan's father wanted to hurt David and that was wrong because David hadn't done anything to deserve that. Jonathan protected David, then had to say goodbye to his good friend.

Who is your best friend? Why do you like him or her? Have you ever stood up for your friend when someone else was teasing him or making fun of him? Has your friend ever done that for you?

Mom's Touch

Good friends make life a lot more fun. Happy times are happier when we share them with a friend and sad times are easier, too.

Share a story with your son about a good friend you had while growing up. Share some of your experiences, especially if one of them shows you or your friend being loyal to one another.

Talk with your son about ways he can show loyalty to a friend. Talk about how a friend will feel if your son stands up for him when others are picking on him. Thank God for the special gift of good friends.

A Verse to Remember

A friend is always loyal, and a brother is born to help in time of need.

Proverbs 17:17

The Real God—

"Make up your minds!" Elijah shouted to the people. He was tired of them claiming to serve God one day, then some fake god the next day. "If God is God, then serve him and forget the others." Elijah was the only one of God's prophets left but the fake god, Baal, had 450 prophets. "Maybe it's time to force the issue," Elijah thought. "I challenge you prophets of Baal to a contest. Meet me on Mt. Carmel and we'll see whose god is the real God!"

The prophets of Baal built an altar and put a bull on it. Then they danced around and called to Baal, "Send fire down and burn up our offering. Come on, Baal . . . yoohoo, Baal!" Elijah leaned against a tree watching this silliness.

Finally, he said, "Maybe Baal is sleeping, or in the bathroom. Maybe he's away on a trip." This just made them shout louder!

After listening to them scream all day Elijah finally said, "Enough already. It's my turn."

He built an altar and put a bull on it. Then Elijah did something strange. He dug a trench around the altar and poured four big jars of water over the whole thing…then he did it again…and again. Water overflowed the trench, the wood and the bull were soaked!

Elijah stepped back and said, "OK God, show these people that you are the true God."

"Ahh! Watch it! Ow, it's hot!" People scrambled out of the way as tongues of fire shot down from heaven and burned up the bull, the altar, and even the water.

"My hair is burned."

"Yuck, that burned meat smells awful!"

The prophets of Baal stared at the smoky remains of the altar. Suddenly one of them shouted, "Let's get outta here!" and they dashed down the mountain. "Grab them!" Elijah shouted. He wasn't going to let them get away with insulting God.

Meanwhile, the crowd of people who had come up to see the contest fell to their knees and bent their faces all the way to the ground. "The Lord is God! The Lord is God!" they shouted.

Based on I Kings 18:19-40

Becoming a Man of God
A man of God takes a stand.

Wow! One man takes a stand against 450 men. Elijah strongly believed in God. He was so sure that God was the real God that he could even make fun of the prophets of Baal when they tried to get Baal to answer them. Those guys could have gotten mad and tried to kill Elijah. But, he wasn't afraid.

Have you ever felt like you should take a stand for God when others were making fun of him? Have you ever heard kids making fun of someone who goes to church or some activity your church is planning? Did you try to stop them? It's not easy to stand up against a crowd, is it?

Mom's Touch

Share a story about some time when you were bothered by people making fun of something or someone. Did you take a stand or not? If not, did you later wish that you had? If you did how did you feel later?

Discuss ways that your son can take a stand for God. He might be able to invite someone to church, or explain to someone why church is important to him. He might be able to explain why he feels some language or activity is wrong because it doesn't honor God. Encourage him to always speak in love and remind him that anytime he takes a stand God is right there to help him.

A Verse to Remember

Those who wait on the LORD will find new strength. They will fly high on wings like eagles. They will run and not grow weary. They will walk and not faint.

Isaiah 40:31

Fly Away Home

"I have so much to learn. I want to be with you every minute," Elisha grabbed Elijah's arm. "I know God wants you to go somewhere. But I want to come with you. Please, don't make me stay behind."

Elisha had a feeling that Elijah wasn't going to be around much longer and he wanted to learn as much as he could from the great prophet of God.

For the next few weeks Elisha follwed Elijah everywhere. He stuck closer than glue! Every time they went to a new town someone would say, "Did you know that God is going to take your master away soon?"

"Be quiet. Of course I know," Elisha always answered. He barely even let himself sleep at night because he wanted to soak up everything Elijah knew and learn from his close walk with God.

One afternoon Elijah and Elisha stopped near the Jordan River. Elisha watched as Elijah carefully folded up his robe. Then Elijah slapped his robe on the waters of the Jordan River. "Wow! The waters are parting!" Elisha was so surprised that he stumbled backwards and fell to the ground. Elijah helped him to his feet and they crossed the Jordan River on dry ground. Elisha wasn't sure what this all meant.

"What can I do for you before I leave?" Elijah asked.

"I want to be God's prophet like you are," Elisha answered.

"That's a tough request. But, if you see me when I'm taken away then you've got it." As Elijah finished speaking a chariot made of fire came between the two men. It was so bright that Elisha had to peek through squinted eyes to see. He was so frightened that he couldn't catch his breath and his heart pounded so loud he was sure everyone could hear it. "Elijah is in the chariot and it's flying away!"

Elisha was so frightened that he couldn't even speak as the chariot disappeared. He stood looking at the sky for awhile then picked up Elijah's robe from the ground. He folded it and hit the waters of the Jordan River with it. They divided, just as they had when Elijah hit them. Then Elisha walked across the river on dry ground and went right past a group of prophets from Jericho who had seen everything that happened. As he passed them, they shouted, "Elisha has taken Elijah's place

Based on 2 Kings 2

Becoming a Man of God

A man of God learns from older Christians.

Elijah had served God for a long time and Elisha knew that he could learn a lot from him. So he stayed very close to Elijah and watched everything he did. What a great way to learn! When Elijah left Elisha knew just what to do, and he showed that by picking up the robe and smacking the waters of the Jordan River.

Who is an older person whom you admire alot? Why? Do you think you could learn things from this person? What kinds of things could you learn?

Mom's Touch

This is a great opportunity to reinforce respect for those who are a little older and have lived a little more life. Share with your son about someone who has mentored you. This doesn't have to be a spiritual mentor, perhaps someone who taught you sports or guided you in developing parenting skills. Talk about what you learned.

Help your son think of older Christians who could help him grow in his Christian walk. What about Christians who could teach him other things like mechanics, fishing, baseball?

A Verse to Remember

And so my children, listen to me, for happy are all who follow my ways. Listen to my counsel and be wise. Don't ignore it.

Proverbs 8:32-33

Olive Oil Overflow

"Momma, what is he talking about?" the little boy asked from behind his mother's skirt.

"Are we going to have to go live with that mean man, Momma?" her other son whispered.

Wasn't it enough that the boys' father had just died? Now this fellow shows up saying that her husband owed him lots of money—and if she doesn't pay up, he will take her sons to be his slaves

"I'm not giving you up, boys," she said. "At least not without a fight." The frightened widow hurried to see Elisha. She knew that if anyone could help her, it would be a prophet of God.

She spilled her story to Elisha and he immediately asked, "What can I do to help you?"

"I don't know," the woman said. "I don't have any money so I can't pay the man what my husband owed. But, all I have left is my sons. Please don't let him take them!"

"Tell me what you have in your house," Elisha said.

"I'm telling you that I have nothing—except one jar of olive oil," she said sadly.

Elisha smiled. "OK, send your sons around to all your neighbors' houses. Have them borrow all the empty jars and bowls they can find."

The woman didn't even ask him why. She sent her sons out to the neighbors right away. When they returned, Elisha told her to take her one little jar of olive oil and pour it into one of the empty jars.

She did what he said. "This one is full. Bring another jar," she called to her son. Jar after jar after jar was filled to the brim from the woman's one little jar of oil. Her sons cheered the awesome miracle!

"Now," Elisha said, "sell all that oil and pay the man what you owe him. There will be enough money left over for you and your sons to buy food."

Based on 2 Kings 4:1-7

Becoming a Man of God
A man of God goes to God for help.

The poor woman in this story was at the end of her rope. Her husband had died. She had no money. She had nothing left but her two precious sons, and now this man was threatening to take them away. But, this woman loved God. She knew that the best thing to do was ask God's prophet for help.

Any problem, any trouble that you might have is best handled by talking to God about it. The great thing to remember is that nothing happens to you without God knowing about it.

When have you had a problem that you didn't know how to solve? Did you talk to God about it? Sometimes a problem seems so bad that it's hard to know how to talk to God about it. That's when it's a good idea to talk to a grown-up like your mom, a Sunday school teacher, or minister. They can help you pray and tell God about it.

Mom's Touch

Tell your son about a difficult situation you have faced—either as a child or an adult. Tell him why it was hard or painful. Tell him how you prayed about it and how God helped you handle the situation.

Tell your son about a time when you just didn't know what to do about a problem. Tell him how you handled that—did you talk with a friend or pastor and discuss how to pray about it or what to do?

Remind your son that God sometimes helps us by showing us what to do, as he did the widow in this story. Sometimes having a great idea is the way God helps us solve a problem.

Ask your son if there is anything he would like you to pray about right now.

A Verse to Remember

If you need wisdom—if you want to know what God wants you to do—ask him and he will gladly tell you.

James 1:5

"We built this room for you to use when you come to town," the nice lady said to Elisha. He sat on the bed and bounced up and down—it was comfortable! He put some of his things on the table. It would be nice to have a place where he could keep stuff and come to rest sometimes. The lady and her husband were extra kind to Elisha. He was very thankful for them.

Later Elisha asked his servant, Gehazi, "What can I do to repay this kind woman. Is there anything she needs?"

"Hmmmm, the only thing I can think of is that she doesn't have a son and her husband is getting very old."

So, Elisha promised the woman that she would soon have a son.

"Oh, don't tease me!" the woman said. She couldn't believe it. But sure enough, about a year later, she had a bouncing baby boy. She was so happy!

The woman loved playing with her son, baking cookies for him, and watching him grow. The little boy loved his mom and adored his dad, following him around and copying everything he did.

One day the little guy was out in the field with his dad when he fell to the ground crying, "My head hurts, owww, my head." A servant carried him to his mom. She did everything she could think of ... but her precious little boy died.

The heart-broken mother lay her son's body on Elisha's bed, brushed his hair back from his eyes and sat with him for a long time. After a while, she knew what she had to do. Hurrying to Elisha she said, "Remember when I asked you not to tease me about having a son. Well, I had my son for just a little while, now he's dead." She cried and cried, holding on to Elisha's feet.

Elisha wanted to send his servant home with the woman to check on the boy. But she cried, "NO! I'm not leaving here without you!"

Finally, Elisha went with her to the boy. He prayed first,
then did a strange thing—he stretched out on top of the
boy—his face over the boy's face, his hands over the
boy's hands. He stayed very still until he felt the boy's body
getting warm. Suddenly the boy sneezed, "Achoo, achoo!"
Seven sneezes and the boy was alive again! "Thank you!"
the happy mother cried. The little boy was not quite sure
what had just happened to him but he was very happy.
The mother, son and Elisha praised God together.

Based on 2 Kings 4:8-37

Becoming a Man of God
A man of God helps others.

Elisha was a busy man. He was a prophet of God so he had a lot of jobs to do and a lot of people to serve. But, Elisha knew this kind woman had a serious problem. Even though he may have been able to help her by just speaking a word or sending his servant, he went home with her because it was important to her to know that he cared that much.

Do you like to help other people? What kinds of things do you do that are helpful?

Mom's Touch

Do you have an example of a time when someone helped you? What did that person do? What did it mean to you? Did it make you feel as if that person truly cared about you?

Think with your son of ways that both of you can help others. Are there things that the two of you enjoy doing together? How can you show people that you care about them?

A Verse to Remember
This is the message we have heard from the beginning: We should love one another.

I John 3:11

Veggie Power

"What makes King Nebuchadnezzar think we'd want to live in the palace? They're acting like it's such an honor!" Daniel and his three friends whispered to one another.

"Yeah, a whole year of training and special treatment ... but we're still prisoners—just prisoners in a palace!" Daniel and his friends were Jewish boys captured by the Babylonians. Because they were young, healthy, and goodlooking they were put in a special training program to become palace workers.

"You will be taught to speak our language. You will be taught the proper way to behave in the palace, and, best of all," the prison guard announced to the group of handsome young men, "you won't have to eat prison food. You will be served the king's best food and wine!"

"Yahoo! Filet mignon! Lobster! Duck L'orange!" the other boys danced around and cheered. But Daniel, Shadrach, Meshach and Abednego weren't so happy.

"That food is offered to idols before it's served to us,"
Daniel whispered to his friends. "We can't eat it because it
would not be honoring to God." The four friends huddled
together and came up with a plan.

"Sir," Daniel addressed the guard very respectfully,
"my friends and I wish to eat vegetables and water
instead of the king's food."

"No way! If you aren't as strong as the other boys
the king will have my neck!" the man shouted.

"Well, how about a test?" Daniel begged. "Give us vegetables and water for 10 days, if we don't look

as good as everyone else after 10 days, we'll eat the king's food." The guard agreed, but he wasn't too sure about this plan.

"Yuck! Why are you eating green stuff when you could have steak and potatoes?" the other boys made fun of Daniel and his friends.

But a strange thing happened. After 10 days, Daniel and his friends were stronger and healthier than all the other boys!

"It's veggies and water for you guys from now on!" the guard laughed. God blessed Daniel, Shadrach, Meshach and Abednego because they honored him. At the end of the training the king was more impressed with these four boys than any of the others.

Based on Daniel 1

Becoming a Man of God
A man of God refuses to compromise.

Daniel and his friends were prisoners. They didn't have any rights at all. It was very brave of Daniel to ask for special permission to eat different food than the other prisoners. Their witness for God was very important to them and they weren't willing to compromise. That means they wouldn't take even one step away from what they believed was the right thing to do. These bright boys came up with a plan to keep from compromising. That was a great idea!

What are some things you know for sure are right? Would anyone be able to get you to change your mind?

Mom's Touch

Wow Mom, this can be a lesson for adults, too, can't it? So many times at school, at work, or in the neighborhood, subtle little things tempt us to compromise our stand for Christ. Share an example of a time you were tempted to compromise, through doing something you weren't comfortable with, or a time when you didn't speak up for God, but knew that you should have. How did you feel—either because you did compromise or you didn't?

What are some ways your son may be tempted to compromise? Can you work together on a plan to solve the problem?

A Verse to Remember

You must love the Lord your God with all your heart, all your soul, and all your mind.

Matthew 22:37

Out of the Frying Pan and Into the Fire

King Nebuchadnezzar thought he was pretty important and he wanted everyone to know it! "This giant 90-foot-tall statue of me is so handsome. I want to be sure everyone notices it." So, the bragging king ordered that anytime his people heard music play, they should bow down and worship his big, golden statue!

"No way am I worshiping this statue," Shadrach declared.
Meshach and Abednego agreed. The three friends loved
God and they knew it would be wrong to even pretend to
worship anyone or anything besides him.

   "Hey!" one of the king's guards poked Shadrach with
his spear. "The king said to bow down and worship the
statue. Are you three gonna hit the ground or what?"

   "No, we're not," Shadrach said calmly.

"These guys refuse to bow to your statue!" the guard
shouted, dragging the boys to the king.

"Is this true?" the king's voice boomed.

Shadrach took a deep breath and stood up tall, "Yes
Sir, we serve God and we will worship only him."

"GUARDS! Heat the furnace up hotter than ever.
We're gonna make some Jewish french fries!" the king
shouted. He was too angry to listen when Shadrach,
Meshach, and Abednego said, "We trust our God to take
care of us."

"So long you stubborn fools!" A guard pushed the three boys into the blazing hot furnace. The fire was so hot that the guard burned to death! But, Shadrach looked over at his friends and they were doing fine. "It's hot alright, but we're not burning up. What's going on? This is strange!"

"Hey, how many guys did you throw in there?" the boys heard the king shouting at his guards.

"Three, your highness."

"Well, then who is that fourth guy in there. He kind of looks like an angel! GET THEM OUT HERE!" King Nebuchadnezzar roared!

Shadrach, Meshach, and Abednego weren't burned at all—they didn't even smell like smoke! "I told you our God would take care of us," Shadrach smiled.

"Yeah, I see what you mean", the king had to admit. "Your God is definitely awesome!"

Based on Daniel 3

"Awesome"

Becoming a Man of God

A man of God believes in God's protection.

The boys in this story believed that God could protect them, even in a blazing furnace. It's easy to trust in God's protection when everything is going fine, but a scary situation like this is where the rubber meets the road.

Hopefully you haven't been in any scary or dangerous situations like these three boys. But someday you may be. The foundation of trust in God is like a tower that has a new layer added every day. What are the ways you see God's care and protection every single day?

Mom's Touch

The boys in this story took a stand for God, and trusted him to do what was best— either protect them or bring them home to be with him. Either choice was fine with them. In today's world our children may be asked to take a stand for God and in some cases that stand may put them in danger. Help your son be ready by teaching him about God's care. Share a story of God's protection in your life, whether supernatural or as normal as being in a car going out of control.

Help your son think of ways God shows him protection every single day. Thank God for his care.

A Verse to Remember

The LORD says, "I will rescue those who love me. I will protect those who trust in my name.

Psalm 91:14

Here Kitty, Kitty

"We have to get rid of Daniel! Did you hear that King Darius wants to make him our boss!"

"Yeah, but why should that Jew be so important here in Babylon? He's just a slave."

The jealous men looked and looked for ways to get Daniel in trouble with the king. But they couldn't find anything—Daniel was squeaky clean! Then one day, "Pssst, hey listen, I have a plan that will cook Daniel's goose. We're gonna trip him up with his own faith!"

"Pssst..."

The sneaky plan was to trick the king into signing a law that people couldn't pray to anyone except him.

Daniel heard about the new law, but he kept right on praying ... to God! "I've talked to God my whole life. I respect King Darius, but I have to do what I know is right." He knelt in front of his bedroom window and poured out his heart to God. Little did Daniel know that his enemies were hiding behind a tree waiting for this exact thing to happen.

The bad guys tripped over each other in their hurry to tattle on Daniel. "Daniel prayed. We saw him!. Throw him to the lions. It's the law, you can't change it . . . ."

"I've been tricked," King Darius moaned. "I'm so sorry Daniel, I have to obey the law," he said sadly.

"Don't worry. God will take care of me," Daniel said. He wasn't even a little bit afraid! The guards threw him into a pit full of hungry lions, then slid a big stone over the top. There was no way out!

It was a long night for the king. He paced around his room worrying about Daniel. "I know when the stone is moved tomorrow all that's left of Daniel will be picked clean bones."

King Darius would have been surprised to know that Daniel was doing fine. God protected him by sending angels to keep the lions' mouths locked tightly shut. They were as gentle as kittens all night long!

At the first peek of morning light King Darius rushed to the lions' den, "Daniel, did your God protect you?" he called.

"Yes, he did!" Daniel called back. "I haven't done anything wrong toward God or you, my king. So he kept the lions' mouths shut!"

"Hurray!" King Darius shouted. "Daniel's God is the real God. Everyone should worship him!"

Based on Daniel 6

Becoming a Man of God

A man of God knows God will do the right thing.

Daniel knew that he hadn't done anything wrong. He obeyed and honored God just as he always did. There was no reason for him to be put to death. In his heart all he wanted to do was worship God and pray to him.

Daniel didn't hide his prayer because he knew that God knew his heart and that he could trust him no matter what.

Have you ever been accused of doing something wrong and had to trust a parent or a teacher to do the right thing? What happened?

Mom's Touch

Things can get a little scary when you must trust someone else to do the right thing on your behalf. Can you share an example of a time when you had to do that? How did it turn out? Can you also share an example of God's justice and fairness on your behalf?

Kids may often feel that they have no control over their lives because adults make all the decisions. Ask your little guy if he feels that way. Talk about ways for him to feel more involved in decisions. Talk about biblical examples of how God always does the right thing so that your son will know he can trust God completely.

A Verse to Remember
God is our refuge and strength, always ready to help in times of trouble

Psalm 46:1

The Fish that Didn't Get Away!

"Nineveh? You want me to go to Nineveh? I don't like those people and if I tell them about you, they might repent of their sins and then—I know you—you would forgive them. No, I won't go!" Jonah stomped around the room and spilled out his anger. God didn't say another word to him. Jonah knew what he SHOULD do ...but he also knew that he was NOT going to Nineveh!

Throwing a few things in a bag Jonah ran for the first ship he saw. "Where you headed?" he called.

"Tarshish," the sailor shouted back. "Great! That's in the opposite direction of Nineveh," Jonah thought. He went straight to the belly of the ship and lay down to sleep. "Hah! Not even God can find me here," he thought as the rocking of the ship lulled him to sleep.

Meanwhile, the sailors had a problem ... "I've never seen a storm blow like this! It came out of nowhere. We're gonna sink. Do something! Throw boxes overboard! Lower the sails! Hurry!" Panicked sailors tossed whatever they could get their hands on—luggage, cargo, even food went into the boiling sea.

Jonah snorted and snored through the whole thing ... until a sailor shouted, "Get up! If you have a god, pray to him cause we've got big trouble!"

Right away Jonah knew what was happening. "Oh man, God found me after all."

"Look, this storm is all my fault—I was hiding from God. Toss me overboard and the storm will stop," Jonah shouted over the roaring wind and splashing sea.

The sailors didn't want to hurt Jonah, but when they realized their choice was to toss Jonah or save their boat, Jonah went flying into the sea.

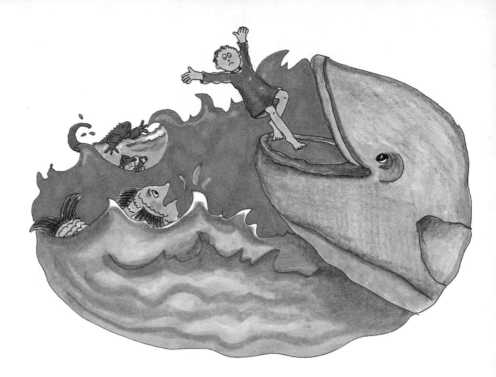

He had barely hit the water when a huge fish swallowed him right down. For 3 days and nights Jonah dodged sea junk in the great fish's belly. "Yuck, I'll never eat fish again!"

Something else Jonah did was think about how he had disobeyed God. He felt bad, "I'm sorry, God. I should have obeyed you. If you still want me to go to Nineveh, I'll go." In a giant burp the big fish spit Jonah onto the beach. Yanking seaweed from his neck and minnows from his ears, Jonah ran for Nineveh.

Based on Jonah 1–4

Becoming a Man of God
A man of God obeys immediately.

Jonah should have obeyed God the first time. Since he didn't he got a free ride in the big fish's belly. But God gave him a second chance and by then Jonah had decided to do the right thing.

How many times has your mom asked you to do something and you have answered, "In a minute!" then you never do what she asked? That's sort of what Jonah did—only he never meant to obey.

When was a time that you didn't obey and were punished? What was the punishment? Did you learn a lesson from this experience?

Mom's Touch

Remember what it's like to be a child? There is always someone telling you what to do. Obeying is a constant challenge. Recall a time when you didn't obey your parents right away. What happened? How did you feel?

Remind your son of a time he did obey you immediately and tell him how proud you were of him. Reinforce obedience every chance you get.

Talk with him about what kinds of instructions he has trouble obeying right away and brainstorm ways you can make it easier.

A Verse to Remember

When you obey me, you remain in my love, just as I obey my Father and remain in his love.

John 15:10

Read My Lips!

"You look like you saw a ghost," a friend said to Zechariah. "Not a ghost—an angel," Zechariah screamed . . . well, he wanted to scream, but when he opened his mouth nothing came out but air! God took away his voice because he didn't believe the angel's message.

Zechariah finished his work at the temple and hurried home to his wife, Elizabeth. He had something important to tell her—if he could make her understand.

"Are you crazy?" Elizabeth had never seen her husband like this. As a priest, Zechariah was normally quiet and kind of stuffy. But here he was jumping around, waving his arms and trying to speak, but no sound came out. "You have something to tell me, right? Just say it!" Elizabeth was frustrated...so was Zechariah. Finally, he grabbed her broom and scratched something in the dirt with the handle. He stepped aside so Elizabeth could read, "We're going to have a baby."

"Now I know you're crazy. You know how old I am. Do you seriously think a baby could grow in this shriveled old body?" Elizabeth grabbed her broom and started back to the house. But when she glanced back at Zechariah's face, she stopped. "You're serious aren't you?" Suddenly her knees felt weak. She had to sit down. "A baby," she thought. "After all these years I'm going to have a baby!"

The next few months were spent getting ready for the blessed event—Zechariah built a cradle, Elizabeth knitted booties. "Come quick!" she would call to Zechariah and he would run to put his hands on her growing tummy and feel their son kick. Sometimes he got frustrated that he couldn't tell his wife how excited he felt about the birth of their child—the special child who would grow up to tell the world that the Messiah was coming!

When their precious baby boy was born all of Zechariah and Elizabeth's relatives came to help them celebrate. Everyone had an opinion of what the baby's name should be. In the middle of the shouting, Zechariah took a tablet and scratched HIS NAME IS JOHN and held it up for all to see. (That's what the angel had said to name him.) Immediately Zechariah's voice came back and he and Elizabeth praised God together!

Based on Luke 1:5-25, 57-64

Becoming a Man of God
A man of God is sometimes quiet.

Zechariah was alone in the temple doing his work as a priest, so it was probably quiet. When he didn't believe the angel's message and God took his voice away it was definitely quiet.

It's very hard to hear God speak, or anyone else for that matter, if you are always making noise.

Do people ever tell you to "Calm down!" or "Use your inside voice!" Why do you think that happens? When someone is trying to explain something to you, do you listen quietly?

A Mom's Touch

More than likely being quiet is not one of your little guy's strong points since most little boys like to make noise. Talk about what he might miss if he isn't sometimes quiet.

Share a story of a time when you didn't listen quietly and you missed some instructions or information. What happened?

If your son does listen quietly tell him how much you appreciate that. Then, go outside together and sit quietly. Listen to all the sounds around you.

Remind your son that God sometimes speaks in a whisper that we hear inside our hearts. If we're always noisy, we might miss what he's saying to us.

A Verse to Remember
Be silent and know that I am God.

Psalm 46:10

A Trusting Step-Dad

"Joseph..."

"Joseph, God knows you are confused and scared. That's OK. He wants you to know that Mary was telling you the truth. The baby she's going to have is the Son of God." Joseph wiggled in his sleep. He didn't usually dream about bigger-than-life shiny white angels—and yet here was one in his dream ... a big one ... and it was speaking to him!

"Oooohhh!" Mary moaned when the donkey stumbled on a stone in the road.

"Are you OK, Mary?" Joseph felt so bad that Mary was bouncing around on the bumpy donkey. She could have stayed home while he went to Bethlehem for the census, but her baby could be born any day and she didn't want to be away from him. "We'll be there soon. Then we'll get a nice hotel room and you can rest," Joseph promised his very pregnant wife.

"I don't feel so good," Mary moaned. Joseph had to admit that the smell of sweaty bodies and dirty animals crowding the streets was sickening.

"Hang on, I'll run in and get a room," Joseph promised, hurrying into the inn. In a few minutes he was back. "It's full. There aren't any rooms left in all of Bethlehem. The best we can get is a spot in the stable. I'm so sorry, Mary." But Mary didn't even care—she just wanted to get off that donkey!

Joseph pulled clean hay from the loft and made a bed for Mary to lie on. She fell asleep right away, even with the cows mooing and the donkey braying. Sometime later she shook Joseph awake, "The baby! The baby is coming!" Poor Joseph wasn't sure what to do, but Mary was so frightened that she didn't want him to leave her to find a midwife. The animals seemed to sense that something special was happening. They were very quiet when Joseph placed the baby boy in Mary's exhausted arms.

In the dim light of dawn Joseph looked up to see some
scraggly shepherds peeking over the stable door. "An
angel told us that your baby is the Messiah. We came to
worship him." It seemed to Joseph that Mary wasn't even
surprised by what they said. Then he remembered the
words of the angel in his dream. "This child will save his
people from their sins."

"It's true," he thought. "The angel's words were true!"

Based on Matthew 1:20-25; Luke 2:1-20

Becoming a Man of God
A man of God trusts God plan.

Joseph and Mary had been planning their wedding for quite a while. All their plans were made and Joseph didn't expect any surprises. But, God had other plans. The news that Mary was expecting a baby was definitely not in their plans. Joseph trusted God enough to continue with the wedding and see what happened.

Have you ever walked into a room that was completely dark? You can't even see your hand in front of your face, let alone where you're walking and whether or not you're going to trip over something? That may be kind of how Joseph felt. He was willing to keep going, even though he didn't really know what was ahead for him.

A Mom's Touch

Share an example of trust from your childhood. Perhaps you had to move to a new town and you had to trust your parents' judgment that everything would be OK. Tell your son how you felt when all you could do was trust someone else—there was nothing you could do yourself about the situation.

Ask your son when he has felt that all he could do in a situation was trust someone else to handle it. Was he afraid? How did it turn out? Build his confidence in God by talking about how he has come through in every situation. Reinforce that God is worthy of our trust because he loves us.

A Verse to Remember

Trust in the LORD with all your heart; do not depend on your own understanding.

Proverbs 3:5

Night ★ Flight

Sometimes Joseph nearly forgot that Jesus wasn't a boy like every other boy. He laughed, slept, burped, spit up, just like any other little one. But the truth slammed into Joseph's heart the day some wise men from another country showed up on fancy camels with

colorful blankets on them. They brought fancy gifts to Jesus and worshiped him. Joseph noticed that Mary was taking everything in, but not saying a word as she cradled Jesus in her arms. "I wonder what is ahead for this little guy," he thought.

A few days after the wise men left the angel visited Joseph's dream again. "Get your little family out of town! Quick! King Herod wants to kill Jesus!" Joseph felt his heart leap into his throat. His stomach hurt and a cold sweat broke out on his forehead. "God is trusting us to raise his son," he thought. "I can't let Herod hurt him!"

HURRY UP!

"Mary, get up. Dress the baby. We have to leave town now," Joseph called. Mary got up and began to pack a few things before she woke the baby. "No! We don't have time to pack. We must hurry. Jesus' life is in danger!" That got Mary moving. In just a few moments she was on the donkey with Jesus sleeping in her arms. Joseph walked ahead of them and the little family disappeared into the darkness outside of Bethlehem.

Joseph, Mary, and Jesus settled in Egypt. "I wonder how long we'll be here," Mary wondered. It was hard to live in a foreign land where the people spoke a different language and their customs were different. The Egyptians didn't even worship God.

Finally, one night the angel came back to Joseph's dream. "King Herod is dead," the angel said. "It's safe to take Jesus home now."

Joseph and Mary were so happy to be able to go home.
They quickly packed the few things they had
accumulated in Egypt. Instead of returning to Bethlehem,
the little family went home to Nazareth. It was so good to
see family and friends again! "Momma, Poppa, I've missed
you so much. This is our son, Jesus!" Mary cried. Finally,
Mary and Joseph could introduce Jesus to their family! It
was good to be home.

Based on Matthew 2:1-23

Becoming a Man of God
A man of God protects.

Joseph could have refused to run to Egypt. He could have said that he would stay in Bethlehem and fight for Jesus' safety. But Joseph was smart enough to know that he should follow any instructions an angel gave him because the most important thing was to protect Jesus from King Herod.

When has your mom or dad protected you? It's a nice feeling to know that someone is keeping you safe, isn't it?

A Mom's Touch

When your children are small you spend a lot of time protecting them from the dangers they don't understand. Share a time when you remember protecting your son. Tell him how very much you love him and how glad you are that he is safe and healthy.

Ask your son if he understands that the rules you make for him are usually for his protection. Talk about ways your son can protect others—a younger sibling or a pet— ways he can show responsibility. Talk about some of God's rules and how they are for our protection. Thank him for his protection.

A Verse to Remember

The LORD keeps watch over you as you come and go, both now and forever.

Psalm 121:8

A Child Shall Lead Them

"I'm so excited!" Jesus could barely sit down to dinner. "I love going to Jerusalem for the Passover Festival. Can I walk with my friends, huh, can I?"

"Hmm, I think you're old enough to walk with your friends this year," Mary smiled. "But sit down and eat dinner now. We still have lots to do before we leave tomorrow morning." Jesus obeyed his mother, as he always did, but it was all he could do to sit still and finish dinner.

" Jesus, over here!"

Early the next morning Jesus was dressed and waiting at the door when his parents got up. Soon they were in the middle of the crowd walking to Jerusalem. "Jesus, over here!" someone called. He ran to join his friends and they laughed and played games as they walked. The Passover celebration was wonderful! Jesus and the other children were quiet and respectful as they and their parents thanked God for taking care of his people.

When the festival ended the tired worshipers headed home. "Have you seen Jesus?" Mary asked.

"No, he's probably with his friends," Joseph answered.

A while later one of Jesus' friends came up. "Where's Jesus?" he asked.

"We thought he was with you," Mary answered.

"No, none of the guys have seen him all day." A stab of fear sank deep into Mary's heart as she shouted, "Jesus is lost!"

Mary grabbed Joseph's hand and they ran back to Jerusalem. They ran until their sides hurt and their breath came in short gasps so strong that they couldn't speak. "He's only twelve. What will happen to him in the big city? How could we lose him?" Mary's panicked heart cried.

For three long days Mary and Joseph searched the city, up and down the streets, every nook and cranny, everywhere they could think to look! Jesus was nowhere to be found!

They had nearly given up when they heard someone mention a boy who was teaching the temple teachers about God. Immediately, Mary and Joseph ran to the temple. It was Jesus! "Do you know what we've been through? We've looked everywhere for you," Mary cried.

Jesus calmly answered, "Didn't you know that I would be in my father's house?" Then he went home with Mary and Joseph. She was so relieved that he was OK that she couldn't stop touching his arm or ruffling his hair.

Based on Luke 2:41-52

Becoming a Man of God
A man of God never gives up.

Imagine the panic Mary and Joseph must have felt. God trusted them to take care of his son ... and they lost him! Immediately Mary and Joseph began searching for Jesus. They looked for one day and they didn't find him, then they looked for another day but they didn't find him. But, Mary and Joseph didn't give up—they kept looking and looking until they found Jesus.

The best things in life take hard work to achieve. Have you ever worked really hard to learn something? Maybe you wanted to give up in the middle, but you didn't, you kept trying and trying until you learned it. Did you feel like celebrating when you finally learned what you had been working on?

A Mom's Touch

Share a story with your son detailing your own perseverance. Tell him about something you had to work constantly to achieve or learn. Let him know how you struggled with it, maybe wanting to give up, but you kept on going.

Remember when you were a child? Big projects or long-term projects sometimes were overwhelming. It was hard to stick with something until it was finished. If you have seen your son stick with a project to completion, compliment him on that perseverance. Talk about areas where he might need to work on sticking with a project. Help him make a plan to do so.

A Verse to Remember

Hold on to the pattern of right teaching you have learned from me. And remember to live in the faith and love that you have in Christ Jesus.

2 Timothy 1:13

Go Fish!

"Would you mind pushing the boat out from shore a bit?"

"Who does this guy think he is?" Peter wondered. "He climbs into my boat and sits down like he owns the world." But, for some reason Peter didn't kick the guy out. In fact, he pushed the boat out just as the man had asked. He went on cleaning his nets while he listened to the man teach the crowd of people on shore. His voice echoed off the water like he was using a loud speaker.

When the man finished teaching Peter expected him to get out of the boat and leave. But, instead the man said, "Go out there where the water is deeper and let your nets down. You'll catch lots of fish."

"Yeah right," Peter thought, a sarcastic smile on his face. "I've been fishing this lake my whole life, and this guy is telling me where to catch fish?"

"Look, my partners and I worked hard all night and we didn't catch a single fish. We're tired— so—thanks anyway but we'll just go on home and get some sleep," Peter said. The man just quietly looked at Peter. For a few minutes Peter seemed to be fighting with himself about what to do. Finally, he took a deep breath and said, "OK. If you want us to try fishing over there, we'll fish over there."

"What's going on?" Peter screamed. He dropped his fishing net into the water and it instantly filled with so many fish that he couldn't pull it up. "Stop!" he called to his partners. "Don't pull any more. The net is ripping! Someone help us! We've got so many fish we can't pull them in."

Peter looked over at the man who had a slight smile on his face. Suddenly Peter knew in his heart that this man was special . . . holy . . . the Son of God!

Peter dropped to his knees—he had never been in the presence of a holy man before. But, Jesus pulled him to his feet, "Don't be afraid," he said. "From now on you will fish for people!" Peter and his partners knew deep in their hearts that Jesus was special. They left their fishing boats right there on the shore and went with him.

Based on Luke 5:1-11

Becoming a Man of God
A man of God follows Jesus.

Jesus has different jobs for each of us to do, because we are each different people. Peter was a fisherman before he met Jesus, so Jesus explained that Peter's work would now be to fish for men, in other words, Peter would tell other people about Jesus and his love. Peter was willing to leave his old life behind and follow Jesus.

Do you need to leave something in your "old life" behind to follow Jesus? Are you ever selfish or grumpy? How about disobedient? To be serious about following Jesus, you must leave those things behind and start a new way of living.

A Mom's Touch

Jesus wants us to follow him and the goal of that following is to bring other people to him. Share with your son the story of who led you to Christ. That person was following Jesus. Tell your son how you share Christ with people, maybe you teach Sunday school, sing in the choir, help a needy neighbor, volunteer in the food pantry, or make friends with people who don't know Christ.

Discuss ways your son can be a "Jesus follower" and tell people about Jesus, either by how he lives his life, or by inviting them to church.

A Verse to Remember

Come, be my disciples, and I will show you how to fish for people!

Matthew 4:19

STORM WARNING

"Man, I'm tired. How does Jesus keep going?" Peter said.

"I don't know, I'm beat, too. But you know Jesus—as long as there are people who want to hear about God, he will keep teaching," John said through a big yawn.

The disciples were sprawled on the ground. Some slept, some chewed on blades of grass. They were listening to Jesus teach and he had been teaching for hours.

"Looks like he's finally wrapping it up," Peter said. "Let's get going." But instead of going to the nearby town, Jesus said he wanted to cross the lake. "I was hoping we could just go to town and get some dinner," one disciple said.

"Shh," Peter whispered. "You know as well as I do that it's best to do what Jesus says." Without another word the disciples climbed into a boat and raised the sail. Jesus went to sleep in the back of the boat.

About half way across the lake the wind picked up and began bouncing the little boat all around.

"Lower the sail!"

"We're taking on water—start bailing!"

The waves tossed fish onto the deck and they flipped and flopped. "Oh wow! We're going down. We're all going to drown out here! WHERE'S JESUS?"

Someone ran to the back and poked Jesus on his shoulder. "Wake up! Don't you care that we're going to drown?"

Jesus stood up and looked out at the big waves, "Be quiet!" he shouted. Instantly the sea was calm again. The wind stopped, the rain stopped, and the waves were gentle.

"Whoa. What just happened here?"

   "How did he do that?"

   Jesus calmly looked around at his friends. "Where is your faith?" he asked. He sounded sad.

   Jesus laid down again, but the disciples kept asking each other, "Who is he? How come the wind and waves do what he tells them to do?"

Based on Luke 8:22-25

Becoming a Man of God
A man of God believes Jesus can do anything!

The disciples were scared even though Jesus, the Son of God, was with them on the boat. They were scared of the storm because they didn't understand that Jesus is more powerful than any storm—or anything else!

What kinds of things scare you? Why do they scare you? Do you talk to God about those things?

A Mom's Touch

Tell your son of a time you were afraid. What frightened you? Was it a storm or an earthquake or maybe just the darkness of a quiet night? How did you get through your fear?

Ask your little guy what he's afraid of. Read the story of Jesus calming the storm again. Remind your son of God's awesome power and constant love. Pray together about the things that frighten you. Thank God that he will take care of you.

A Verse to Remember
The LORD is king! Let the earth rejoice!

Psalm 97:1

Bread and Fish for Everyone!

"Mom! Jesus is in town teaching about God! Can I go? Mom, please, can I go?" the little boy bounced up and down around his mother.

"Well, I guess so, but let me make a lunch for you."

"Oh, Mom, I don't need a lunch," the boy whined, edging toward the door.

"Oh, right. You're 'starving' every ten minutes, and you don't need a lunch. It will take me five minutes!"

"Wow! There's thousands of people here!" the boy thought as he picked his way through the crowd. He found a spot close to the front and sat down to listen. No one said a word for hours as Jesus talked about God's love. Pretty soon one of Jesus' helpers said, "It's late, Master. Send the people home for dinner."

"NO!" if the boy were braver he would have shouted, "I don't want to go yet. Please Jesus, keep teaching!" He almost cheered out loud when Jesus said, "No. You give them dinner."

"We don't have any food, and no money to buy it," the man argued.

"Sir, you can have my lunch if you want," the little boy held up his small bundle.

Jesus' helper sneered at the little lunch, "That won't do any good with all these people!"

The little boy hung his head feeling dumb for thinking his little lunch could help."

A gentle hand slowly lifted the boy's chin. Jesus smiled as he took the little lunch and prayed, "Thank you, God, for this food."

Then he broke the bread and fish into pieces and the disciples passed it out to the people. They kept coming back and Jesus kept giving them more and more. "How did he do that?" the boy wondered, munching on his second helping.

Jesus' helpers walked through the crowd, picking up leftover food. "There must be five thousand people here! Everyone ate all they wanted and there are twelve baskets full of left-overs!" The boy's skin prickled like someone was watching him. He looked around and saw Jesus smiling at him! "Wow! Just 'cause I shared my lunch I got to help with a miracle!"

Based on John 6:1-13

Becoming a Man of God
A man of God shares

When the little boy brought a lunch that day he had no idea he was going to be able to help with a miracle. When he heard that Jesus needed food for the people, the little boy gave his whole lunch. He didn't take out some for himself or hold some back. He shared it all.

Do you have something that you don't like to share? Maybe it's a favorite toy or book? How do you feel when a friend doesn't share with you?

A Mom's Touch

Mom, tell your son a sharing story—a time when someone shared something special with you and how you felt about that person after that. Tell about a time when you shared, or didn't share and how you felt afterward.

Encourage your son to share generously. Point out a time when you noticed him sharing and tell him how proud you were of him.

A Verse to Remember
Do for others what you would like them to do for you.

Matthew 7:12

# Ghost Man Walking?

"Hey, do you see something out there on the water?"

"Yeah, it looks like some kind of sea monster."

"Nah, it's a ...ghost!"

"Oh, come on. Get real."

"Well, then what do you think it is? There's something out there. Even in this storm I can see something." The disciples leaned out over the water and squinted their eyes, trying to make out what the thing was.

John shivered a little, "I wish Jesus was here. I always feel better when he's with us."

"Yeah, me too. And besides whatever is out there, this storm is getting pretty bad. I hope our boat doesn't take on much more water."

"Oh boy. That thing out there is getting closer! You'd think with this storm blowing so hard we'd be all the way across the lake by now." John pushed Peter in front of him and hid behind the big fisherman's back.

"It's a ghost! Oh God in heaven, protect us!" Even big brave Peter squeezed his eyes shut in fear.

"Hey, don't be afraid. It's me!" Peter opened one eye and saw what looked like Jesus walking on top of the stormy water.

"Jesus, if it's really you, let me walk to you on the water!" Peter was climbing out of the boat as he shouted.

"All right. Come on."

Peter almost ran across the top of the water until a big wave smacked him in the face. Suddenly he realized, "What am I doing?" At that very instant, it felt like the top of the water cracked and Peter quickly dropped into it. "Help! Help me!" he splashed and kicked and coughed.

Jesus pulled him up and as Peter coughed and gasped Jesus said, "You don't have much faith, do you? Why didn't you believe I could keep you safe?"

The other disciples helped Peter and Jesus climb into the boat. When they were safely inside, the wind suddenly stopped blowing. Stars glittered in the night sky, shining on the quiet sea.

Each of the tired men dropped to his knees in awe and worship. "This man really is the Son of God," one of them whispered.

Based on Matthew 14:22-33

Becoming a Man of God
A man of God keeps his eyes on Jesus.

Peter jumped out of the boat and started walking on the water. He did fine as long as he kept his eyes on Jesus. But the minute he started looking around at the waves and the storm he started sinking—he took his eyes off Jesus, the one who could keep him safe.

Some things, like hitting a baseball can't be done unless keep your eyes on what you're doing. If you take your eyes off the ball and swing the bat—you miss the ball. How good are you at keeping your eyes on what you're doing, no matter what else is going on?

A Mom's Touch

Share with your son some activity you did as a child that required focus. Did you play a sport such as tennis, basketball, baseball, or did you play a musical instrument, or do needlepoint? All those activities require staying focused and keeping your eyes on what you're doing.

Talk with your son about how important it is to keep our eyes on Jesus. How do we keep our eyes on him? By reading God's Word and learning about him and by praying and listening for him to speak to us.

A Verse to Remember

Praise the LORD, I tell myself, and never forget the good things he does for me.

Psalm 103:2

Little Man,  Big Change

"Get out of my way! Move it! Come on, I want to see Jesus, too!" Zacchaeus pushed and shoved, but no one moved to let the little man through.

"What's the matter with you people? Don't you know who I am?" That was the wrong thing to say. Tax collectors like Zacchaeus were not popular because they cheated people out of their money.

"There he is. There's Jesus." The words rolled through the crowd and people pushed closer to the road. Someone pushed Zacchaeus back, then an arm came from nowhere and slammed him against a tree. That tree gave Zacchaeus an idea. He scooted up it and out to the edge of a big branch just in time to see a crowd of people come down the road. "That man in the middle must be Jesus," thought Zacchaeus.

Shouts of, "Jesus, give me . . . help me," grew louder as the crowd got closer. Finally, the crowd passed below the branch where Zacchaeus sat. He had a bird's eye view!

Zacchaeus nearly fell off the branch when Jesus looked up at him and said, "Zacchaeus, come down. I want to come to your house."

"He knows my name," the little man thought in amazement. He jumped down, brushed the dust from his clothes and proudly led the way to his house.

Zacchaeus strutted down the street, proud as a peacock.
He wanted to be sure everyone knew that Jesus wanted
to come to his house! "Ha! Jesus didn't ask to come to any
of your houses," he seemed to be bragging.

"Why is Jesus going with that cheater?" people
complained. "He doesn't deserve to have Jesus spend
time with him!" The little man ignored every comment and
proudly opened the door to his fine home.

As Jesus and Zacchaeus talked, the tax collector understood how wrong it was for him to cheat people of their hard-earned money. "I promise to give half of everything I own to the poor. And I will pay back the people I cheated. In fact, I'll pay back four times more than I owe!"

Jesus smiled at the little man. He knew that Zacchaeus would never be the same. He loved God now and he would treat people honestly!

Based on Luke 19:1-10

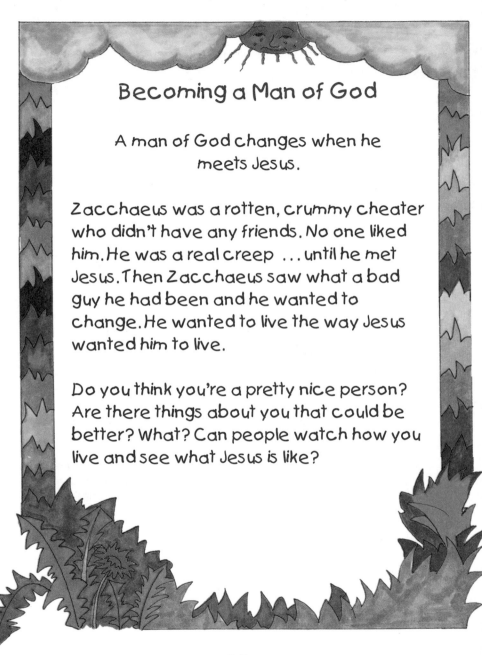

Becoming a Man of God

A man of God changes when he
meets Jesus.

Zacchaeus was a rotten, crummy cheater
who didn't have any friends. No one liked
him. He was a real creep ... until he met
Jesus. Then Zacchaeus saw what a bad
guy he had been and he wanted to
change. He wanted to live the way Jesus
wanted him to live.

Do you think you're a pretty nice person?
Are there things about you that could be
better? What? Can people watch how you
live and see what Jesus is like?

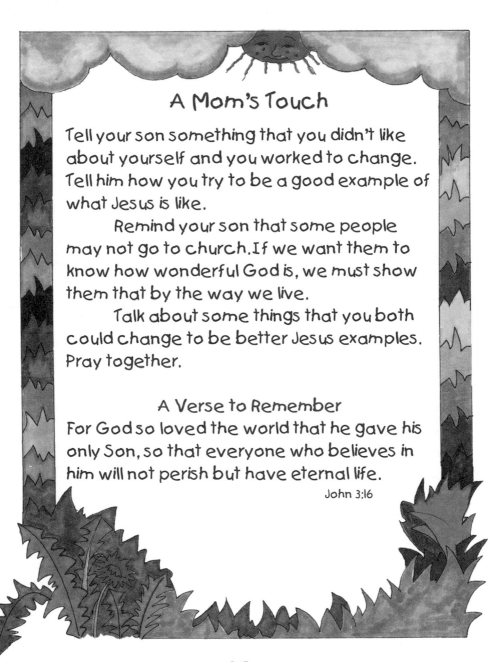

A Mom's Touch

Tell your son something that you didn't like about yourself and you worked to change. Tell him how you try to be a good example of what Jesus is like.

Remind your son that some people may not go to church. If we want them to know how wonderful God is, we must show them that by the way we live.

Talk about some things that you both could change to be better Jesus examples. Pray together.

A Verse to Remember
For God so loved the world that he gave his only Son, so that everyone who believes in him will not perish but have eternal life.

John 3:16

Dad Always Liked You Best

"I'm sick and tired of this farm! I want more excitement! Bright lights and city life are for me!"

"Quit complaining and get busy. We have to get this fence mended today," the older brother was tired of his younger brother's whining and even more tired that he had to constantly nag him to get his work done.

"Well, you can stay on this farm 'til you rot, but I've got a plan and I'm going to be out of here quicker than you can say, 'Hand me a hammer!'"

That evening the young son had a talk with his father. "Dad, I need more excitement than I get watching wheat grow. How about if you give me my inheritance now? Then I can move to the big city and have some fun!"

His father sadly gave him the money and watched his young son leave home. The minute the boy hit the city, he started spending—fancy restaurants, big parties, gifts for his new friends. In no time at all the money was all gone.

"I left home to get away from farm stuff. Now the only job I can find is feeding pigs. What stinks is that they have food to eat and I don't! I hate to do it, but I'd better crawl back to Dad on my hands and knees and ask if he will let me be one of his hired hands. I don't deserve to be his son anymore. I've made some bad choices!"

When the boy got close to home, his father ran to meet him. "You're home! Hurrah! I've been waiting for you!" The boy tried to ask about being a hired worker. But, he couldn't get a word in edgewise.

"Cook a fancy meal. Put a purple robe and gold ring on the boy. My son is home and we're going to party all night!" The boy had never seen his dad so happy!

Meanwhile the older son worked away out in the fields. He heard music and laughter up at the house and came home to see what was going on. When he heard about the party he said, "I've been stuck here—doing my work and my brother's. I'm not going to a party for him! No one ever threw a party for me, even though I've been the good son all this time!"

The servant told the father about the older boy's feelings. The father went to see his son, "Don't you understand? I thought your brother was dead, but now here he is—alive and well. Best of all, he's home. I have to celebrate!"

Jesus told this story to show an example of how God forgives us for doing wrong things and welcomes us back to him.

Based on Luke 15:11-32

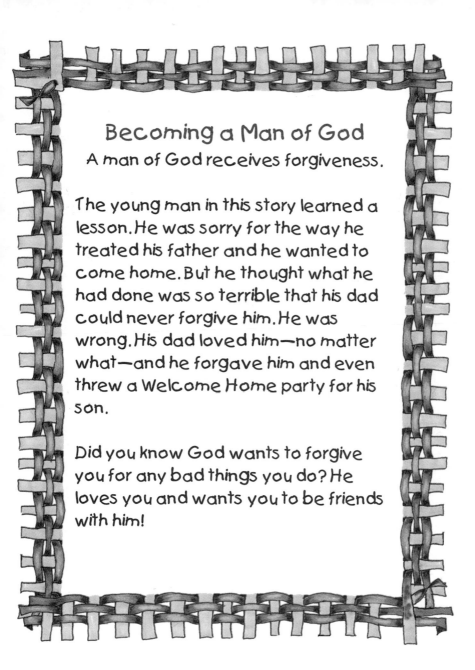

Becoming a Man of God

A man of God receives forgiveness.

The young man in this story learned a lesson. He was sorry for the way he treated his father and he wanted to come home. But he thought what he had done was so terrible that his dad could never forgive him. He was wrong. His dad loved him—no matter what—and he forgave him and even threw a Welcome Home party for his son.

Did you know God wants to forgive you for any bad things you do? He loves you and wants you to be friends with him!

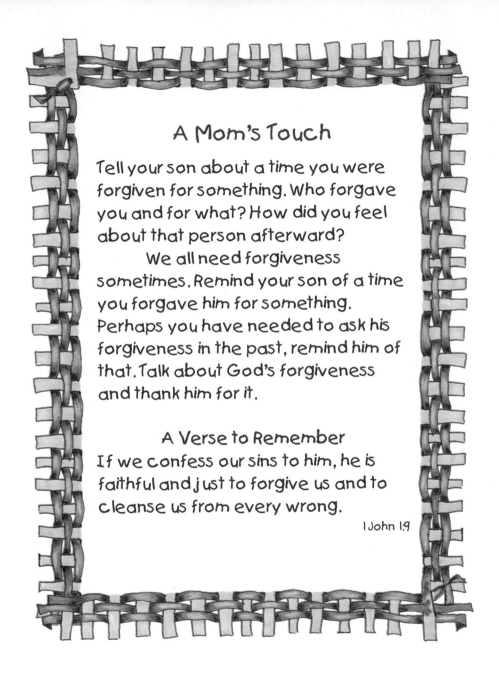

A Mom's Touch

Tell your son about a time you were forgiven for something. Who forgave you and for what? How did you feel about that person afterward?

We all need forgiveness sometimes. Remind your son of a time you forgave him for something. Perhaps you have needed to ask his forgiveness in the past, remind him of that. Talk about God's forgiveness and thank him for it.

A Verse to Remember

If we confess our sins to him, he is faithful and just to forgive us and to cleanse us from every wrong.

1 John 1:9

A Friend In Need is a Friend Indeed

"What a nice day for my walk to Jericho," the man thought. He walked slowly, enjoying the sunshine, smelling the sweet flowers. He didn't pay much attention to the fact that he was the only person on the road. He was sorry he hadn't when a couple of creeps jumped out from behind a rock and knocked him down. "Let me up!" he screamed. But one of the robbers hit him on the head with a rock and left him bleeding on the side of the road. When he woke up, his money was gone, his clothes were gone. They even took his shoes!

"They just left me on this deserted road to bleed to death. That's just what is going to happen, too," he thought. When he heard footsteps later, he struggled to lift his head. "Hurrah! A priest. If anyone will help me a priest will."

But to his surprise the priest looked at him with disgust, "Ugh! Why is this piece of garbage in the road!" Then he crossed the road and kept right on walking.

The sun beat down on the poor man. He had nearly given up hope when he once again heard footsteps. This time he didn't have the strength to lift his head, but squinting through half-opened eyes, he saw a temple worker coming toward him. The poor man lifted his hand and weakly called, "Help me. Please help me!" The temple worker came up to the man and poked him with his toe. "Hmm, this fellow has been beaten up pretty bad," he thought, "but I'm busy. I've got work to do." He stepped over the man and kept right on walking.

It was nearly dark before the man heard more footsteps.
This time he didn't even open his eyes until he felt a gentle
hand lift his head and slide a pillow under it. "A Samaritan.
Samaritans hate us Jews. Why would you stop to help me?
Do you think you're going to rob me? Sorry, buddy there's
nothing left," the hurt man thought, closing his eyes.

He must have gone to sleep because he woke up to find that he was lying in a soft bed in a nice inn. The Samaritan was cleaning his cuts and putting bandages on them. Then he saw the good Samaritan give the innkeeper gold pieces to take care of him. The man sighed and let himself relax. He knew he didn't have anything to worry about now.

Jesus told this story to make people think about who they should be helping.

Based on Luke 10:30-37

Becoming a Man of God
A man of God doesn't have favorites.

The priest and the temple worker in this story wanted to only help people who were just like them. That's not the way to show God's love, is it?

Do you know any people whose skin is a different color from yours, or people who speak a different language than you? Do you know people who live a different way than you do? People who are poorer or richer than you? Did you know that God loves them, too?

A Mom's Touch

Share a story with your son of the first time you took a chance and befriended someone who was different from you. How was the person different? Did you become friends and have fun playing together? Have you ever observed prejudice first hand? Talk about how that made you feel.

Does your son know people of different races or cultures? Talk about how he feels about them. Has he ever witnessed prejudice?

A Verse to Remember

Love each other. Just as I have loved you, you should love each other.

John 13:34

A Heartbroken Mom

"Momma, I don't feel so good," the little boy crawled up on his mom's lap. She rocked him, singing softly and holding a cool cloth on his hot forehead.

Even though the loving mother did everything she could think of, her little boy got sicker and sicker. "Oh God, my son is the only family I have left. My husband has already died. Please don't take my boy," she prayed, kneeling at his bedside.

Even with her constant attention, the little boy died. Heartbroken, the mother sat beside her dead son's bed. She held his hand and thought about how he used to run and play and laugh and tease.

Friends came over with food and flowers. But the sad mom didn't even talk to them. Finally, her friends started making funeral arrangements. They thought she was so heartbroken she would sit beside the boy's body forever if they didn't take charge.

On the day of the funeral one of her friends actually took her hand and led her out of the house to go with them to bury her son. Friends lifted the boy's coffin to their shoulders and the crowd of family and friends followed along behind them. The sad parade walked through town, people on the streets stopped and looked at them, feeling bad for the sad mother.

At the city gate the little funeral procession waited while people came through, then a group of men stepped aside to respectfully let the funeral  pass. The men thought, "It's not hard to see who the mother of the dead boy is. Grief shows all over her. She can barely walk, her head is bowed to the ground and tears are raining on her feet." Suddenly one man stepped out of the crowd and gently took the woman's hand. "Don't be sad," he said quietly. The people around her thought the man was crazy. How could the woman not be sad that her son was dead?

But they all knew that the man was Jesus when he took the dead boy's hand and said, "Get up!" To everyone's amazement, the boy sat up. Alive! His surprised mother nearly fainted. Jesus still held her hand in his and he gently pressed her son's hand into it. In no time at all the happy woman was laughing, crying, and hugging her live son. But, she didn't forget to thank Jesus for giving her son back to her.

Based on Luke 7:11-17

Becoming a Man of God
A man of God thanks God for all he does.

Wow! Imagine how excited that momma must have been. The thing she wanted so very much—but never dreamed would happen was done for her! She probably couldn't say thank you enough times.

Do you like to be thanked when you help someone or do a job for someone? Don't you think God would probably like to be thanked, too?

A Mom's Touch

Tell your son about a time when you worked hard on something and got a big "thank you". How did you feel? Tell him about a time when you worked hard on something and didn't get any thanks at all. How did you feel then? Which person did you want to help again?

Tell your son about a time when you heard him say, "Thank you" without being reminded to do so. Tell him how proud you were of him.

Pray together, thanking God for all he's done for you . . . especially for giving you each other!

A Verse to Remember

Give thanks to the LORD and proclaim his greatness. Let the whole world know what he has done.

I Chronicles 16:8

"Doves for sale. Get your sacrificial birds here!" Urgent cries offering deals "too good to pass by" rang through the normally hushed and respectful temple. Signs hung from the grand columns advertising "Change your money to Temple Coins here —25¢ on the dollar!" Hardly a fair price for a working man's money!

Jesus couldn't believe it as he pushed his way through the heavy crowds. "Simple Jewish people come here to worship God, but the temple is so noisy and smelly...how can anyone even think of God? And these men selling doves and changing money—they are trying to get rich by people's worship!"

With every step Jesus took he felt more frustrated, "This is not the way to treat God's house!" Walking up to a money-changer's table, Jesus swiped his arm across it and coins went flying every which way. Shouts of, "What do you think you're doing?" rang out, but Jesus ignored them and started turning tables upside down. Arms grabbed at him from every which way, trying to pull him to the floor, but he seemed to have a super-human strength that kept him going.

"This is God's house–my father's house–and it is to be a place of prayer. It is not a place for you to make money by cheating people who come to worship God." Jesus worked his way up the aisle, turning over table after table, scattering doves and spilling money. Each time someone tried to stop him, he stared at him with such fierceness that the man backed away in fear.

When the floor was covered with coins and birds were
flapping all over the temple, the merchants ran, afraid of
what Jesus would do next. But he was finished now, so
Jesus sat down. Quickly, people surrounded him, begging
for healing. Children climbed into his
lap. Shouts of, "Praise God for the Son
of David!" echoed through the
temple. The jealous Pharisees
began talking among
themselves about how
to get rid of Jesus.

Based on Matthew 21:12-17

Becoming a Man of God

A man of God respects God's house.

Jesus felt very strongly that God's house was a special place for worship. He wanted it to be treated with respect. Even if some people didn't come there to worship, he didn't want them to bother the people who did want to worship.

What is your church like? What is your favorite part of the service? Are you quiet and respectful when you go into the church? Do you sit quietly in the church service so people around you aren't disturbed?

A Mom's Touch

Tell your son what the church you attended as a child looked like. Was it far from your home? Did you have friends there? Was it large or small? How did people dress on Sunday morning? What was the service like?

Talk about the proper way to behave in God's house. If your son does behave respectfully in church, compliment him. If he has trouble being respectful in God's house, talk about some ways to make it easier.

A Verse to Remember

I was glad when they said to me, "Let us go to the house of the LORD."

Psalm 122:1

Through the Roof

Every day was exactly the same for the man. His legs didn't work so he lay in bed all day ... every day. He couldn't get his own breakfast, go to work, or even pick up something he dropped. The highlight of his day was when one of his good friends walked through the door. "That's one thing I have to be thankful for," the man often thought. "I have wonderful, helpful friends."

Four of the man's good friends often stopped by to talk.
They laughed and remembered the old days when he
went fishing with them, or played a game of catch.

   One night the friends left the crippled man in bed
and started home. "Wish there was something we could
do to help him," one man said. That started everyone
talking ... soon the four friends came up with an incredible
plan ... that just might work!

The next day they were all back at their friend's house. One of them carried a cot that had a handle at each corner. "One, two, three," they shouted and at the count of three they lifted their crippled friend onto the fancy cot.

"Where are we going?" the man asked. But his friends just told him to lean back and enjoy the ride. They carried him through town—he saw places he hadn't seen in years—to a little house crowded with people listening to Jesus of Nazareth teach about God's love.

"Coming through!" the men shouted, trying to part the crowd and get their friend to Jesus. But, instead of moving aside, the crowd moved closer together. Everyone wanted to see Jesus—and they weren't letting anyone cut to the front of the line!

"Well, that's that," thought the crippled man. "At least my friends tried. I know Jesus could heal me if he wanted to, but not if they can't get me to him." However, the four friends didn't give up so easily, they huddled together and came up with Plan "B".

The men grabbed the cot and ran to the rooftop. "What are you doing?" he cried, holding on for dear life. No one answered. They dug at the grass and tiles on the roof, keeping at it until there was a hole big enough to lower his cot into the room—right in front of Jesus.

The gentle teacher looked up at the four friends peering through the hole in the roof. When he saw their faith in him, he said to the crippled man, "Get up and walk." He did! Dust and dirt showered everyone in the room as four happy men danced on the roof.

Based on Mark 2:3-12

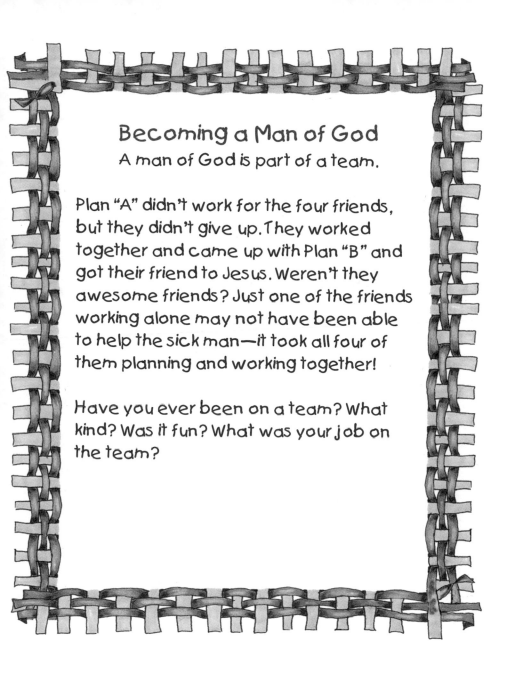

Becoming a Man of God
A man of God is part of a team.

Plan "A" didn't work for the four friends, but they didn't give up. They worked together and came up with Plan "B" and got their friend to Jesus. Weren't they awesome friends? Just one of the friends working alone may not have been able to help the sick man—it took all four of them planning and working together!

Have you ever been on a team? What kind? Was it fun? What was your job on the team?

A Mom's Touch

Tell your son about a team experience you have had. Were you on a soccer, baseball, or speech team as a child? Perhaps you played in a band or sang in a choir—that's a team effort, too. Tell him how the team worked together and what your part on it was.

Discuss how God's family must work together as a team and how each part is important. God has given us all different gifts and each is necessary to get his work done.

A Verse to Remember
All of you together are Christ's body, and each one of you is a separate and necessary part of it.

I Corinthians 12:27

282

Devoted  Sisters

"Mary, it's your turn. Come on, get up now," Martha whispered. The sisters were taking turns sitting up with their sick brother, Lazarus. Martha sat through the night, gently laying cool, wet cloths on Lazarus' feverish forehead. In the daytime Mary gently fluffed his pillows and tried to think of ways to make him more comfortable.

Lazarus had been sick for several days and Martha tried
all the home remedies she knew. No matter what the
worried sisters did, Lazarus got worse.

One afternoon when Mary went to town to buy food
she heard that Jesus was in a nearby town. Mary ran all
the way home to tell Martha. "Jesus is close by. Let's send
for him. I know he can help Lazarus!" The sisters sent a
message to Jesus right away. "Lazarus is very sick. Please
come quickly!"

One day passed, then two ... Mary and Martha waited eagerly for Jesus to come. Meanwhile, Lazarus' condition got worse and worse ... then one night he quietly died.

"Why didn't Jesus come?" Mary asked through her tears. Martha sadly shook her head. She, too, wondered why Jesus hadn't come. She kept herself busy making arrangements for her brother's funeral, but her heart was confused and hurting.

A few days later a friend ran into the house and
breathlessly reported, "Jesus is coming."

"Now he comes—when Lazarus is dead and buried.
Where was Jesus when he could have helped my
brother?" Martha dried her hands and went to meet Jesus.
Her frustration spilled out at him. Mary couldn't believe
how her prim and proper sister was speaking to the great
teacher. "If you had been here, Lazarus wouldn't have
died. That's the bottom line!"

Jesus wasn't upset at Martha. He asked, "Where is Lazarus buried?" They led him to the tomb, wondering what he was going to do. "Open the tomb!" Jesus commanded.

"No! Lazarus has been dead for four days, it will smell terrible in there!" Martha gasped.

But Jesus waited while the stone was moved then he called, "Lazarus, come out!" Mary closed her eyes and hid behind Martha, until she heard "oohh" escape from her sister's lips. She looked up and saw Lazarus standing in the tomb door—alive and well!

Based on John 11:1-44

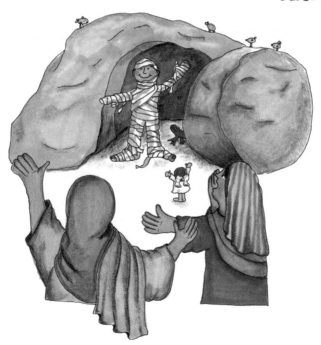

Becoming a Man of God
A man of God tells God how he feels.

Mary and Martha told Jesus how they felt. They were disappointed and they didn't try to hide it. They knew that Jesus could take it. Jesus wants us to be honest with him, he knows our hearts anyway, so we might as well just tell him how we feel. We can tell him when we're disappointed or hurt. He won't stop loving us. Honesty is the best policy.

Have you ever been disappointed or sad about how God answered a prayer or handled a situation. Did you tell him?

A Mom's Touch

Does your son feel he can be honest with you? If he feels he has been unjustly punished or accused, can he tell you?

Share a time from your childhood when you felt unjustly punished or accused. Did you tell your parents or teacher? What happened?

Talk about telling God your true feelings. Why is it scary to do that? Why is it OK to do so? Does God know how we feel anyway? Pray together and thank God that you can be honest with one another and with him.

A Verse to Remember
The LORD is close to all who call on him.

Psalm 145:18

A DARK DAY IN HISTORY

Mary's face flushed red and little beads of sweat popped out on her forehead. She felt a faintness creeping up from her stomach to her head so she grabbed a friend's arm to steady herself.

When a Roman soldier slapped a whip across Jesus' back, Mary flinched. She moved to the back of the crowd, but kept her eyes on Jesus. "Get moving!" the soldier shouted. Jesus hoisted the wooden cross to his shoulder and walked slowly down the road.

Mary's heart ached as the crowds of people shouted at her son and made fun of him, "Yeah, look at the king of the Jews now!" "Why don't you call an angel army to save you?" She looked away. It was just too heartbreaking to see what they were doing to Jesus.

The gruesome parade reached the hill called Calvary and
the soldiers threw Jesus to the ground and
nailed his hands and feet to the wooden
cross. When they dropped the cross
into the ground, Mary pushed her
way to the front, standing right
below Jesus. Jeers rang out, "Come
on King of the Jews. Save yourself. Where's all
your power now?"

The man on the cross was kind and loving. Mary had known him for his whole life and he had never done anything wrong or even unkind. Mary also remembered almost 34 years ago when the angel told her that she was going to have a baby and that he would be the Messiah—the one who would save his people. This must be what the angel meant.

Mary looked into Jesus' eyes—the eyes
of her son—the eyes of God's son.
Despite all the terrible things happening to him this day his
eyes were filled with love, complete and total love, even
for the people killing him and making fun of him.

It was the oddest feeling for Mary when Jesus lifted
his head and said, "It is finished." When he died, part of her
heart died too ... and yet she knew she was reborn at that
moment ... into the family of God.

Based on John 19:16-30

Becoming a Man of God
A man of God understands Jesus died on the cross for him.

A loving momma would do almost anything to help her son. But, there wasn't anything Mary could do about this. This was why Jesus came to earth. Jesus left the riches of heaven to come to earth and live as a poor man. He was not treated very nice by some people. They finally killed him on the cross, just like a plain old thief, even though he hadn't done anything wrong. He was willing to go through all of this because he loves us so much.

Have you ever been blamed for something you didn't do? Did you just take the punishment or loudly announce that you were innocent?

A Mom's Touch

Tell your son about a time when he was sick or hurt and how bad you felt for him.

Before Jesus died on the cross, people had to sacrifice an animal, such as a sheep or a dove to God before they could ask him to forgive their sins. Explain to your son that we don't have to do that anymore because Jesus died on the cross as the sacrifice for our sins. Thank him for this wonderful gift!

A Verse to Remember

Christ died for everyone.

2 Corinthians 5:14

The Empty Tomb

The sun was just peeking over the horizon when three women began a quiet walk to the cemetery. Each woman walked with her head bowed, shoulders slumping. All of their hope had died when Jesus died. Their world turned upside down that day. Jesus taught them so much about God, but then he died—could they believe anything he said? Each woman felt a dull aching pain in her stomach.

Did the sun come up today? Was the sky still blue? Were flowers still colorful and sweet? You wouldn't know by looking at any of these women. Even in the middle of their pain the women wanted to do the right thing—that's what they had been taught their whole lives. So, they were going to anoint Jesus' body with oil and perfumes because that was their custom. But their hearts didn't feel anything except empty numbness.

The women had known each other for years, shared joys and sorrows, prayed together, but today none of them knew what to say. So, they walked in silence until one of them remembered the big stone. Several soldiers had strained and pushed to roll it in front of the tomb door. "How are we going to move that stone?" the woman wondered aloud. Her friend dropped the basket she was carrying, "How much more do we have to go through before this is all over?" she spouted in frustration.

"Come on, we'll figure something out," the third woman encouraged. As they rounded the bend before the tomb, the woman in front suddenly stopped. Her friends, walking with bowed heads, bumped right into her.

"Its ... gone!" she whispered. "The stone is gone, the tomb is open." The women looked at each other as fear rose in their throats. What could this mean?

The bravest of the three women stumbled into the open tomb. She fell to her knees when a voice said, "I know you're looking for Jesus. He's not here. He is alive. He came back to life just as he said he would."

"He's alive! He's alive!" the woman shouted to her friends. "Praise God! Praise God! Jesus is alive!"

Based on Mark 16:1-7

Becoming a Man of God
A man of God knows God will do what he says.

The poor women going to the tomb were so sad they didn't know what to do. That's because they had forgotten what Jesus said he would do—or they didn't believe it. Jesus said he would come back to life, but they sure weren't expecting it when they went to the tomb that morning.

Has someone ever told you that something would happen, but you didn't believe it? If it did happen, how did you feel? If it didn't how did you feel?

A Mom's Touch

Share some of your hopes for your son's future. Share some of the hopes you had as a child. Did any of them come true?

Explain that the women at the tomb that morning had given up hope because they didn't know that Jesus would do what he said. When they found out he was alive and that he had done what he said, they were very, very happy. Thank Jesus for coming back to life and that you can someday be in heaven with him.

A Verse to Remember

You are looking for Jesus, the Nazarene, who was crucified. He isn't here! He has been raised from the dead!

Mark 16:6

No Leg to Stand On

Every day was the same for the man. His friends carried him to the same place near the Beautiful Gate of the city of Jerusalem. Sometimes they complained about having to take him there. On those days, they dropped him off quickly, then ran before he could ask them to do anything else. Crowds of people poured in and out of Jerusalem every day. He had a good spot for begging there by the Beautiful Gate.

Day in and day out the man begged money from the
people going in and out of Jerusalem. That's the only way
he could earn any money. His legs didn't work so he
couldn't get a job. He was a pushy man—that's why
people sometimes didn't want to be around him. He
seemed to feel that healthy, strong men owed him
something and he made it his purpose in life to get every
cent from them that he could.

This day started out like any other day ... the trip to the Gate, his friends running away, his constant begging. "Come on—you can spare some change for a crippled old man!"

"Sir!" a voice interrupted the stream of begging. He looked up to see who was speaking to him, but the bright sun blinded him so that he couldn't make out the faces of the two men standing in front of him.

He waited for one of the men to drop coins into his metal cup, instead the same voice said, "I don't have any money to give you."

"Then move out of the way. Let the paying customers in," the beggar's voice dripped with sarcasm.

"Wait, I have something better than money," the voice said again. The old man couldn't imagine anything better than money, but he was interested in what the stranger was talking about. So he waited, "In the name of Jesus of Nazareth, get up and walk!" the stranger said.

The man started
to snap a sarcastic
slam about how ridiculous
this comment was. Except,
he felt a strange tingling in
his legs and feet. He had
never felt ANYTHING in his
legs and feet. Dead muscles
zoomed to life, crooked
bones straightened. Peter took the
man's arms and lifted him to his feet.
His legs held him up! Joy and gratitude
flooded through his body and spilled from
his mouth. "Praise God! Praise God!" he
shouted, running, and jumping, and kicking his
heels together.

Based on Acts 3:1-10

Becoming a Man of God
A man of God desires God's best.

The beggar in this story wanted money. That's as far as his dream went. He didn't dare hope for anything better. He almost missed receiving God's wonderful gift of healing because he wasn't thinking that big. He set his goals too low.

What's the best gift you ever received? What was the best surprise gift you ever had?

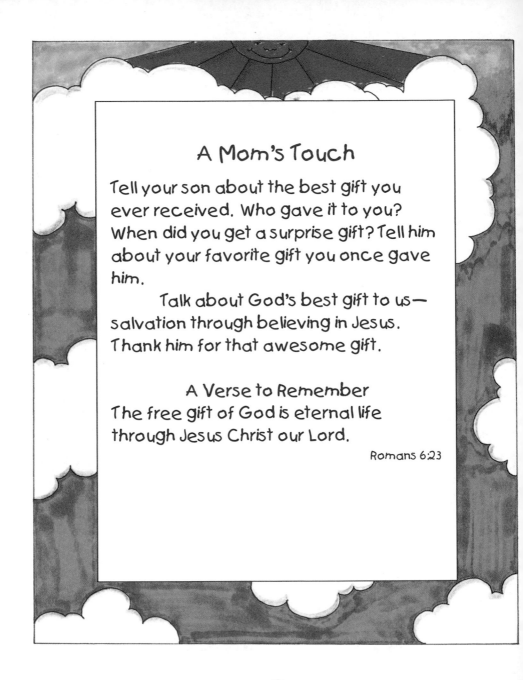

A Mom's Touch

Tell your son about the best gift you ever received. Who gave it to you? When did you get a surprise gift? Tell him about your favorite gift you once gave him.

Talk about God's best gift to us— salvation through believing in Jesus. Thank him for that awesome gift.

A Verse to Remember

The free gift of God is eternal life through Jesus Christ our Lord.

Romans 6:23

One Hundred Yard Dash....

"Philip, go south down the desert road that goes from Jerusalem to Gaza." Philip didn't even question the order—when the angel of God tells you to do something, it's best to just do it! He turned around and started walking toward Gaza, even though he didn't know why he was going there.

After a while a fancy carriage came barreling toward him. Philip stepped off the road so it wouldn't hit him. As it passed he saw that a man from Ethiopia was inside. "He must be important in the government judging from the markings on his carriage," Philip thought. The carriage was a good way down the road when the Holy Spirit told Philip to run along beside it. Again, Philip didn't question, he just broke into a fast run and caught up to the fancy chariot. Running along beside it, he heard the man inside reading from the book of Isaiah.

"Do you understand what you're reading?" Philip called to the man. The Ethiopian was surprised that a man was jogging along beside his chariot.

"No," he answered. "How can I understand it unless someone explains it to me. Are you saying that you understand it?"

"Well, yes. I can tell you what it means." So the man stopped his carriage and Philip climbed in.

"These verses are talking about Jesus of Nazareth," Philip
explained. He used other verses he knew too, about why
Jesus came to earth, how he was killed, but came back to
life and lives in heaven making a way for all who believe in
him to come to heaven someday. Philip told the Ethiopian
the whole story of God's wonderful love.

"Stop the carriage! Stop!" the man shouted. "Look, there is some water over there. Why can't I be baptized right now? I believe what you are telling me about Jesus."

Philip and the man went into the water and Philip baptized him. As he lifted the man out of the water, God took Philip away and the new believer never saw him again, but he praised God all the way back to Ethiopia.

Based on Acts 8:26-40

Becoming a Man of God
A man of God shares God's love with others.

Philip had information that would help the man in the chariot understand God's Word. He was willing to share that information even though he had to change his plans to talk to the man.

Who explains God's Word to you? Have you shared God's Word with anyone?

A Mom's Touch

Tell your son about a favorite Sunday school teacher or pastor from your youth. Why did you like this person so much? Did you learn about God's Word from this person? Did your mom or dad share God's Word with you?

Ask your son if there is anything about God's Word that he doesn't understand. If so, talk about it or make plans to discuss it with your pastor together.

A Verse to Remember

Your word is a lamp for my feet and a light for my path.

Psalm 119:105

A Changed ♥ Heart

"Christians! I hate them!" Every time Saul even said the word "Christian" he got a bad taste in his mouth and a knot of hate formed in his stomach. "I'm getting rid of all Christians if it's the last thing I do!" Just about the only thing that brought a smile to Saul's face was standing outside the jail and making fun of the Christians he had thrown in there.

After years of hunting down Christians and throwing them in jail, Saul felt he had taken care of all the Christians in Jerusalem.

"My work here is done. I think I'll go to Damascus and get rid of the Christians there, too." Saul and some of his friends began the walk to Damascus. Shortly after they began the trip, Saul heard a voice say, "Saul, why are you persecuting me?" He stopped and looked around but didn't see anyone.

"Saul, why are you persecuting me?" This time a blinding light shot out of the sky and shined directly on Saul. He fell to the ground and crawled on his hands and knees trying to get away from the light. But the light moved right along with him and the voice kept asking, "Saul, why are you persecuting me?"

For once, Saul's know-it-all friends were speechless. They heard the voice but couldn't figure out where it came from. Wisely, they didn't try to tell Saul what to do.

Finally Saul understood that whoever was speaking was not going away. "Who are you?" Saul asked softly. He wasn't sure he wanted to know.

"I am Jesus, the one you are persecuting."

Saul hung his head, "It's true then," he thought. "Jesus is real. The Christians have been right all along. I'm the one who has been wrong." Right there on the dusty road to Damascus Saul told Jesus he was sorry for everything he had done.

In that instant, Saul's heart was changed. He no longer
wanted to hurt Christians, now he was a Christian, too.
God changed Saul's name to Paul. Saul's life was devoted
to getting rid of Christians—Paul's life was devoted to
winning people to Christ.

Based on Acts 9

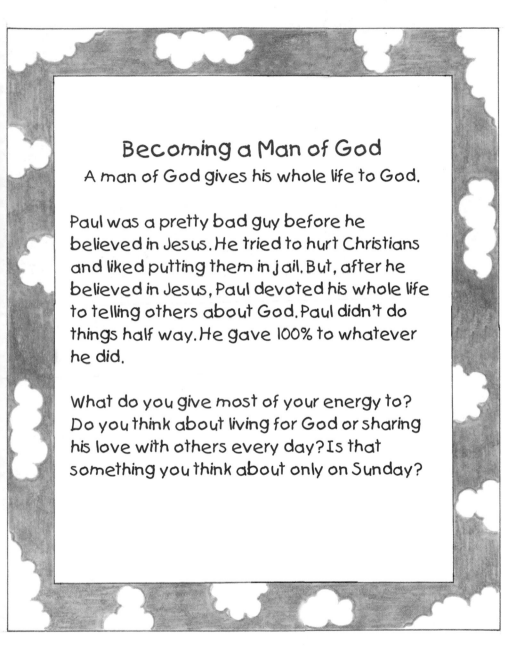

Becoming a Man of God
A man of God gives his whole life to God.

Paul was a pretty bad guy before he believed in Jesus. He tried to hurt Christians and liked putting them in jail. But, after he believed in Jesus, Paul devoted his whole life to telling others about God. Paul didn't do things half way. He gave 100% to whatever he did.

What do you give most of your energy to? Do you think about living for God or sharing his love with others every day? Is that something you think about only on Sunday?

A Mom's Touch

Mom, share your conversion experience with your son. What were you like before meeting Jesus? How were you different afterwards? Tell him how living for God is part of your everyday life. Does he know if you pray daily, or have daily devotions? Does he hear you speak of God daily?

Pray together that you will both make God part of your lives every single day.

A Verse to Remember

Draw close to God, and God will draw close to you.

James 4:8

A Special Escort

"I'm so tired," Peter thought. "If I could just get a little sleep...." However, it's kind of hard to sleep when you've got chains on your legs holding you to two guards, one on either side. The three of them did settle down on the cold floor of the prison cell to try to get some rest. But one of the guards snored so loud that Peter couldn't sleep. He just laid on the floor and watched ants crawl over the guards' legs.

"I'm not even sure why I'm in prison anyway. I guess it's just because I'm a Christian and I teach about Jesus Christ." Peter thought about his friend James. King Herod had murdered him and the people laughed and cheered. Soon after that Peter was arrested. He wondered what King Herod had up his sleeve for him. Just then the sleeping guard snorted. Peter rolled him over onto his side and propped his own leg against him. The chain cut into his shin, but the pain was better than the snoring.

Late into the night Peter finally fell asleep. He had nightmares about what was going to happen to him—he knew that 4 squads of 4 soldiers each were standing guard outside his cell so there was no chance of escape.

Peter's sleep was restless. He wanted to toss and turn, but the chains held him still. Then in the middle of his dream about shouting crowds and guards with spears a bright, bright light shined into his cell. It was brighter than any light he had ever seen.

Peter woke up when something sharp jabbed him in the ribs. "It can't be morning already," he moaned. The two guards were still snoring away. "I must be dreaming," Peter thought. That's when he saw a glowing angel standing in front of him.

"Get up and get dressed," the angel said. Peter started to point out that the chains held him tight—but suddenly the chains dropped off. The angel led Peter out of the cell, through the prison, past guards who didn't even seem to see them. Finally, they were standing safely on the street outside the prison.

"Hey, thanks . . ." Peter started to say, but the angel disappeared as quickly as it had come. Now Peter knew for sure that he wasn't dreaming this prison escape.

He hurried to a house where he knew all his friends were praying for his safety. At first the servant girl was so shocked that she forgot to let Peter in. "Oh no," he thought. "I'm not just going home. I have to tell my friends about the miracle God did to keep me safe." When she finally let him inside, Peter led the little group in praising God.

Based on Acts 12:1-9

Becoming a Man of God
A man of God prays for others.

What awesome friends Peter had! He was in serious trouble and they really cared about him, so they stopped everything they were doing and met together to pray for him. It's a real privilege to pray for our friends and family members. God promises to hear our prayers and answer them.

Do you have a list of family members or friends for whom you pray? Do you know if there is someone praying for you? If so, how does that make you feel?

A Mom's Touch

Do you know of someone who prayed for you daily when you were a child? A parent or grandparent? If so, share how that made you feel.

Do you pray for your children on a daily basis? Tell your son that you do. Tell him what kinds of things you pray for him. If you know that God has answered some of your prayers for your son, tell him about that.

Show your son how to make a prayer chart, listing requests, praises, and answers to prayers.

A Verse to Remember

The earnest prayer of a righteous person has great power and wonderful results.

James 5:16

Shake and Break

The jailer shoved Paul into the damp, dark cell. It was buried in the very center of the prison. Roaches and ants scurried across the floor as Paul fell onto it.

Paul had been in prison before, but this time he and Silas were in big trouble. The jailer had strict orders to be sure they didn't escape.

"All I did was set a young girl free from the demon that controlled her," Paul thought. "You'd think people would cheer that and thank me for saving her." Instead Paul and Silas were beaten with sticks and whips, then thrown into prison. Paul remembered not so long ago when he made it his business to beat Christians with whips and chains. He had thrown them in prison and laughed that they would never see the light of day again.

Now, he and Silas sat on the filthy floor with their feet in chains. "You know Silas, the other prisoners here need to know that God loves them," Paul said.

"Right, and we have a captive audience," Silas agreed. They began singing songs of praise to God. At first the other prisoners thought they were crazy, then they began to listen to the words Paul and Silas sang.

Many men leaned back against damp walls and listened to the comforting songs. Around midnight the walls and floor of the prison started shaking, almost like a large army was riding into town. Then the shaking got worse and Paul and Silas held onto each other. The floor lurched sideways and Paul was tossed across the room. The chains on his legs broke off. He was free! A grinding crack broke through the screams as the cell doors splintered and broke open. Prisoners started to run away, sure that the earthquake was their ticket to freedom.

The jailer struggled through piles of stones and broken chains to see his jail completely destroyed. Thinking all his prisoners were gone he drew his sword to take his own life. "Stop," Paul shouted. "Don't hurt yourself. We're all here."

The jailer couldn't believe that Paul and Silas kept all the prisoners there when they all could have escaped. "Sir," he asked, "can you tell me how to be saved?"

Based on Acts 16:16-40

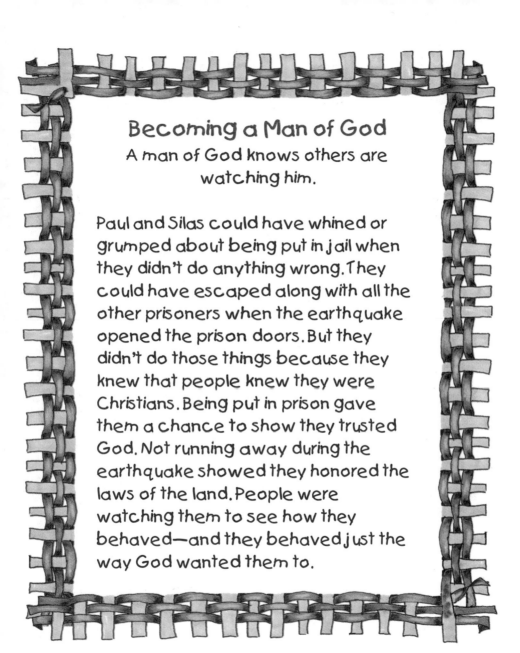

Becoming a Man of God
A man of God knows others are watching him.

Paul and Silas could have whined or grumped about being put in jail when they didn't do anything wrong. They could have escaped along with all the other prisoners when the earthquake opened the prison doors. But they didn't do those things because they knew that people knew they were Christians. Being put in prison gave them a chance to show they trusted God. Not running away during the earthquake showed they honored the laws of the land. People were watching them to see how they behaved—and they behaved just the way God wanted them to.

A Mom's Touch

Can you recall a time when you didn't behave in a way that was a good example of how God wants you to behave. Can you recall a time when you did? How did you feel after each of these experiences?

Reinforce your son's good behaviors by pointing them out and telling him how proud you are of him. Point out specific behaviors such as kindness or honesty and remind him how those behaviors show non-Christians what God is like. Remind him that he isn't too young to be an example of God's love to others.

A Verse to Remember
Be an example to all believers in what you teach, in the way you live, in your love, your faith, and your purity.

I Timothy 4:12

Shipwreck!

"I demand to go to Rome! I am a Roman citizen and I have a right to be tried by Caesar himself," Paul was very firm about what he wanted. He knew that he had done nothing wrong and there was no real reason for his arrest. The only complaint against him was that he was a Christian and preached about Jesus Christ. He had a better chance for a fair trial in Rome than he did in Caesarea.

"Move it!" the guard jabbed his spear at the line of prisoners filing onto the big sailing ship. Chained together the prisoners couldn't move too quickly, but the guard paid no attention to that problem. "I said to get going!" the crack of his whip against some poor man's back made all the prisoners try their best to move a little faster.

One morning a strong wind blowing across the sea sent the sailors into a panic. "Storm coming! Batten down the hatches, tie down the cargo! Move it!" Whips cracked across prisoners' backs as they pushed to get set for the storm.

Paul heard the sailors' panic, "This is a northeaster if I've ever seen one! We're taking on water. The ship is going to go down!"

The prisoners bailed water as fast as their chains would allow them to move, but the ship kept sinking lower and lower in the water. "Lighten her load. Throw over the cargo. Throw anything that's loose!"

Days at a time the sailors bailed water and fought the storm, not even taking time to eat.

"Stop worrying!" Paul shouted over the wind. "Go eat something. Most of you haven't eaten for two weeks. You've got to keep your strength up! God told me in a dream that the ship will sink. But, we will all be saved. Trust him!"

The other prisoners and the sailors thought Paul was crazy . . . and they kept right on bailing water. Later the ship hit some rocks and broke into a million pieces, but every man on the ship; prisoners, sailors, guards made it safely to shore—just as God said they would.

Based on Acts 27:13-44

Praise God!

Becoming a Man of God
A man of God stays calm in a crisis.

Everyone on the ship was going crazy except Paul. The sailors and prisoners all thought they were going to die. But Paul trusted God and God said that he would take care of everyone on the ship.

What kinds of things make you afraid or nervous? Do you relax if your mom tells you everything will be OK, or do you keep on worrying?

A Mom's Touch

Does your son know that you are sometimes nervous or afraid? Tell him what kinds of situations worry you. Tell him how you handle those fears and how you give them to God and trust him to take care of them.

Talk about your son's fears and encourage him to trust God with them. Memorize verses that remind him of God's care. Encourage him to say the verses or sing choruses about God's love and care when he is afraid.

A Verse to Remember

Give all your worries and cares to God, for he cares about what happens to you.

I Peter 5:7

An Evil Plan

"Listen to me! I've got nothing to apologize for. I've tried to live my life the way God wants me to! I am on trial just because I believe that we can live in heaven someday." Paul always said exactly what he thought. But, this speech to the High Council made the religious leaders angry. Suddenly a fight broke out between the Pharisees who agreed with Paul and the Sadducees who didn't.

"He's wrong," some shouted.

"He's right," others screamed.

The man in charge thought the men were going to rip Paul into pieces. "Put Paul in prison!" he shouted, "Otherwise these men will kill him!"

The next morning a group of more than 40 Jews held a secret meeting, "We promise that we will not eat or drink until Paul is dead!"

"He is going down! We will have the leaders bring him back to the Council for more questions. On the way there will be a mysterious ambush—and Paul will be dead. Is everybody in?"

"Yeah! Right! We're in!" cries rang out and fists shook in the air.

The group didn't know that a young boy stood outside the doorway of their secret meeting room. He heard their whole evil plan.

The boy quietly slipped away from the door and ran to the prison. Outside one tiny cell window he knelt on the ground. "Uncle Paul, Uncle Paul," he called. Paul came to the window, glad to see his nephew. The young boy told his uncle about the plan to kill him. Paul knew what to do.

"Sir," Paul called one of the prison officials. "Please take this boy to the commander. He has important information that the commander needs to know."

The young boy wished his uncle would just tell the man about the plan. "It's too scary to talk to the commander. I'm just a kid," he thought. But, he knew that his uncle's life depended on his courage. So, he went to the commander and shyly told him about the Jews' plans—and even how he was part of it because they wanted him to send Paul back to the High Council for questioning.

The commander listened to the boy's story, asked a few questions, then leaped into action. "Get two hundred soldiers ready to leave for Caesarea tonight. Also two hundred spearmen and seventy horsemen. Get horses for Paul to ride and take this letter to Governor Felix. Paul must be in Caesarea by morning!"

The young boy felt proud that he helped save Paul's life and ruined the evil plans of the hungry, thirsty Jews.

Based on Acts 23:1-35

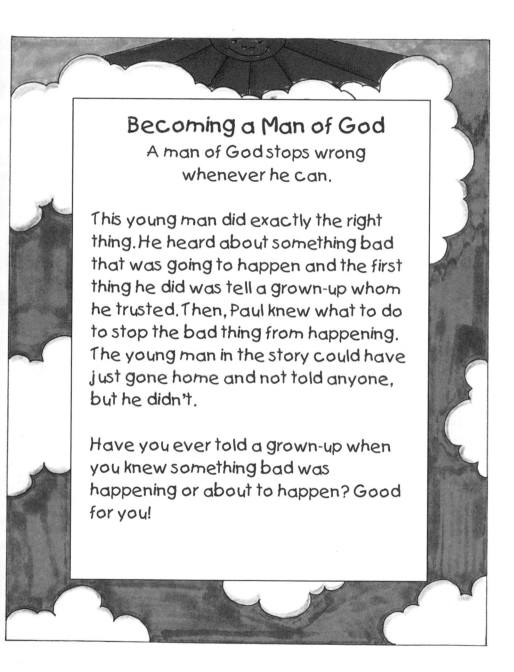

Becoming a Man of God
A man of God stops wrong whenever he can.

This young man did exactly the right thing. He heard about something bad that was going to happen and the first thing he did was tell a grown-up whom he trusted. Then, Paul knew what to do to stop the bad thing from happening. The young man in the story could have just gone home and not told anyone, but he didn't.

Have you ever told a grown-up when you knew something bad was happening or about to happen? Good for you!

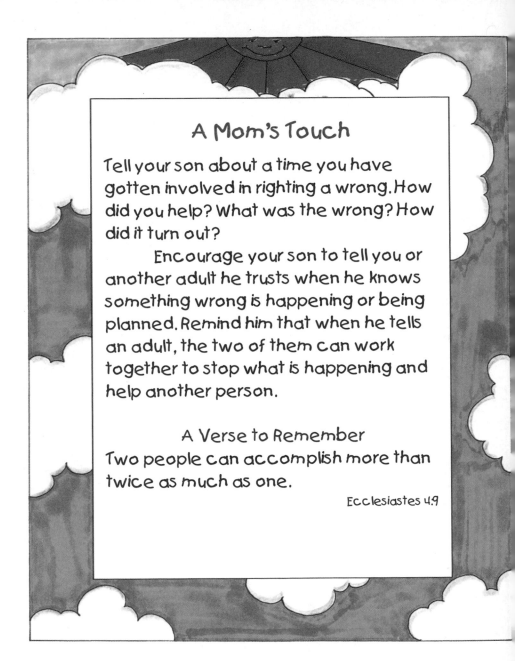

A Mom's Touch

Tell your son about a time you have gotten involved in righting a wrong. How did you help? What was the wrong? How did it turn out?

Encourage your son to tell you or another adult he trusts when he knows something wrong is happening or being planned. Remind him that when he tells an adult, the two of them can work together to stop what is happening and help another person.

A Verse to Remember
Two people can accomplish more than twice as much as one.

Ecclesiastes 4:9

The Holy City

The apostle John was a friend of Jesus. He traveled with him, and heard him teach, and saw him do amazing miracles. He also saw Jesus die on the cross. Jesus asked John to take care of his mother, Mary. John loved Jesus— and Jesus loved John.

When John was an old man God sent an angel with a special message for all people who love God. John wrote it down in a special book called Revelation. This is part of John's message:

Revelation

1 This book unveils some of the future activities soon to occur in the life of Jesus Christ. God permitted him to reveal these things to John in a vision; and the

JOHN

A new city will come down from heaven...

...and God's people will live with him.

The old world full of bad people and bad things will disappear someday. A new city will come down from heaven and God's people will live in it with him. This city will be more beautiful than anything you can imagine. It will sparkle like diamonds on a sunny day. Walls that are wide and tall will surround the whole city.

Each side of the wall will have three gates in it. Each gate is named for one of the twelve tribes of Israel and a beautiful angel will stand guard at each gate.

The wall of this beautiful city will have twelve big foundation stones, one named for each of Jesus' special friends, the disciples.

The city will be made of pure gold—gold that is as clear as glass. The foundation stones of the wall will each have beautiful gem stones in them like emerald, onyx, topaz, and amethyst. The twelve gates will be made of pearls—big, big pearls. Each gate will be one single pearl!

There will be no need for a sun or moon in this beautiful city, because God's light will fill it. Nothing bad will be allowed inside, no sadness will be there either.

John wrote about the holy city so that God's children can look forward to being there someday—with Jesus and with everyone who loves him!

Based on Revelation 21

Becoming a Man of God

A man of God knows heaven is
waiting for him.

Isn't it exciting that God told John these
wonderful things about heaven? It's exciting
to think about heaven and being there with
God someday, isn't it? God has planned a
beautiful place filled with love and singing
and complete happiness for his children.

Do you think about what heaven is like? Do
you know anyone who has already died and
is with God now?

A Mom's Touch

Tell your son about loved ones who have already died, and whom you will see again in heaven some day. Talk about rewards and how rewards are given for jobs done well—winning a race means you get a ribbon or trophy, studying hard for a test means you get a good grade. Heaven is a wonderful reward for God's children. Ask your son what he things heaven will be like.

Pray together and thank God for heaven and for making a way for us to be with him there.

A Verse to Remember

All who are victorious will inherit all these blessings, and I will be their God, and they will be my children.

Revelation 21:7